WALKING THE SCOTTISH HIGHLAND ROUND

A 13-STAGE, LONG-DISTANCE ROUTE TAKING IN THE BEST OF THE SOUTHERN AND CENTRAL HIGHLANDS

STEPHEN WHITEHORNE

WARD LOCK

A WARD LOCK BOOK
First published in the UK 1999
by Ward Lock
Wellington House
125 Strand
LONDON
WC2R 0BB

A Cassell Imprint

Distributed in the United States
by Sterling Publishing Co., Inc.
387 Park Avenue South, New York, NY 10016-8810

A British Library Cataloguing in Publication Data block for this book may be obtained
from the British Library

ISBN 0 7063 7521 1
Designed by Grahame Dudley Associates
Printed and bound in Slovenia by DELO-tiskarna d.d.
by arrangement with Korotan Ljubljana d.o.o.

To Virginie

'Mountain thoughts river feelings – never betray them.'
(YAN WAN-LI, TWELFTH-CENTURY CHINESE POET)

ACKNOWLEDGEMENTS

Once again, I am indebted to Virginie, not only for her continued support and tolerance of my countless unreasonable requests but, more pragmatically, for her typing and computer skills.

Virginie, Simon Mootz and Emma Cadzow have all been great companions on the hills over the last year or so and have somehow managed to endure my repeated interruptions with the dictaphone and the camera. I thank them for their friendship and their patience.

While I was researching the Highland Round, Tam Bolton of the Luib Hotel made some useful suggestions regarding possible routes over the Crianlarich hills, and the local knowledge of Kenneth Briggs at GlenView was vital when I came to finalizing a feasible ascent route from Glen Etive to Bidean nam Bian, while the advice of the warden at Killin Youth Hostel was especially helpful about a practicable high-level route between Killin and Luib.

The cloud that burst over the hills on the afternoon I stumbled upon the Rannoch Station Tearoom proved to have a silver lining. Mrs McLellan – who serves great tea and cakes on the platform – was able to give me details on just about all the possible accommodation in the area.

For sowing a seed of inspiration, I am grateful to Tom Lawton for his book *Walking the Lakeland Round*, and finally, I thank the publishers for allowing that seed to germinate in Scotland.

The quote on page 164 is from *The Four Quartets* (T.S. Eliot, published by Faber and Faber Ltd).

CONTENTS

PREFACE

The philosopher George Steiner has pointed out that as we enter the third millennium, the luxuries we will come to value most are silence and space. To many people, such a realization seems already pertinent, and noise pollution and the tranquillity-famine of urban living are probably the catalysts for many of our weekend exoduses to the Scottish hills.

The forces that threaten our physical, psychological and spiritual breathing spaces are diverse, but top of the list for many is probably the fact that too few places are safe from the all-pervading effects of the motorcar. It is likely that few of us could name more than half a dozen places where road traffic can be neither seen nor heard, and now no hillside, moorland, forest or animal is safe from the ubiquitous four-wheel-drive and bull bar. Perhaps in the Scottish Highlands, however, more than anywhere else in Britain, opportunities to escape and breathe are, thankfully, still numerous. After a spell of living and working in the Highlands some years ago, I am now once again based in a city, although a return to sanity is just a couple of hours away.

The celebrated beauty of Scotland's mountain landscape is manifest in many ways and is undoubtedly magnified by the solitude and peace that, military jets aside, still pervade much of the wilderness. Each year more visitors recognize these qualities, and the area becomes increasingly valuable as a recreational resource. Tourism is now Scotland's biggest industry, which, on the face of it, would itself seem to be a safeguard against any spoiling of the land, the very thing that people come to enjoy. However, an unfortunate irony remains – tourism will always destroy its objective – and there are many examples from around the world to support that proposition.

As an author of walking guides, I am, perhaps, guilty of encouraging further pressures on the land. Yet I have never believed that the cause of the conservationist is best served by restricting access to wilderness. A love and respect for the land can only flourish when an attachment to it, a familiarity with it and a freedom to embrace it are fostered. And so, in a sense, it is the pursuit of these goals that has motivated me in my efforts to devise this Highland Round.

My hope is that the Highland Round will not be considered merely a physical challenge and I would discourage the 'Scout Master' approach to walking it. For reasons of safety, it is, of course, vital to set off armed with a level of mountaineering skill appropriate to the challenge, but obsessional name-ticking, bagging and quantifying can too often obscure the more profound pleasures of the Scottish mountains. Those of us who feel, as John Muir put it, 'that going to the hills is going home', might love a favourite mountain for the mystery of its landscapes, the poetry of its natural history or perhaps even for the capriciousness of its climate. As another Victorian, W.H. Hudson, wrote in 1900 in *Nature in Downland*: 'This silence of the hills does not impress one at once if the mind is occupied with thinking, or the eyes with seeing.'

Embrace the Highland experience in all its dimensions. When heading out over the hills, recognize that each person's perception of the Highlands has as much to do with the imagination as it does with geography. Mountains are landscapes of the mind, and even in the geographical sense, overfamiliarity is unlikely. So make time for contemplation, pack your attitude along with your maps and enjoy the Highland Round.

STEPHEN WHITEHORNE

Concept of the Highland Round and Practicalities

Most walkers who set off to explore the Scottish mountains do so by following routes that start and finish from the same place and that can be completed in a single day. A convenient parking place is, for most, an important consideration. Long-distance routes of several days' duration are undoubtedly becoming more popular, however, and the demand for new and sustained challenges continues to grow among the walking fraternity. In Scotland one has only to point to the phenomenal success of the West Highland Way (WHW) for evidence. Apart from the WHW, there are in Scotland two other designated long-distance footpaths – the Southern Upland Way and the Speyside Way. A fourth route, the Great Glen Way, is currently at an advanced stage of planning. Each of the 'Ways' has been conceived to start at one point and to finish at another; in the case of the Southern Upland Way, these points are over 320km (200 miles) apart. Such linear routes have received criticism in the past for having too many sections with little of interest to see. I believe that my Highland Round represents an innovation in Scotland, in being the only circular long-distance route yet to have been devised and published.

The Highland Round is certainly not a well-defined unbroken footpath from start to finish (or, rather, from start to start), and I hope it will never become so. Throughout, I have planned the route with flexibility and sustained interest in mind. The remote nature of some places demands the frequent traverse of unpathed terrain, and while I have described in some detail an 'ideal' main route, I have also outlined various alternatives to suit a range of weather conditions, or walker's ability or inclination.

The Highland Round is a challenging route that includes some of Britain's highest mountains and can be walked over consecutive days, making it an excellent fortnight's holiday. Alternatively, it can be walked over several weeks, months or even years. I have tried to achieve as varied and complete an impression

8

of the mountain landscape, nature and character of the Central and Southern Highlands as is possible in two weeks, and the criteria I applied in devising the route are that each stage:

❖ must be capable of completion by hillwalkers of reasonable fitness in a single day;

❖ must finish each day at or near appropriate accommodation, which will also be the start point for the following stage;

❖ must have a high-level option on low-level days and vice versa;

❖ must require no rock climbing and provide an easier alternative wherever scrambling is involved.

If walkers use the suggested accommodations each night they will not have to carry camping equipment and, laden with little more than a day sack, they are therefore guaranteed maximum mobility and enjoyment. While I was researching and planning for the Highland Round, first finding and then combining the accommodation with the best of the area's mountains, lochs and glens proved to be immensely difficult. The Scottish Highlands are today far less densely populated than they once were, and the problems I had no doubt reflect the far-flung distribution of settlements in the region.

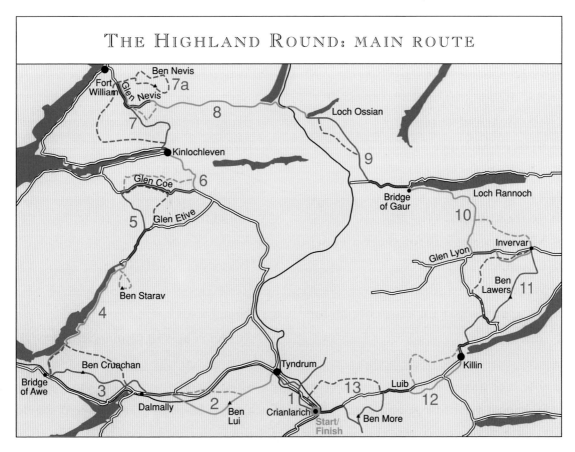

THE HIGHLAND ROUND: MAIN ROUTE

The Highland Round is especially suited to fit and experienced hillwalkers, who may have undertaken long-distance walking routes in the past. Before undertaking the Round, walkers should have gained some previous experience on the Scottish mountains, perhaps by having climbed a few Munros. Those walkers who lack this level of familiarity with the terrain should first tackle a few of the easier stages as day routes, progressing later to routes on the high mountains. It is probable that those most likely to engage in the challenge that is the subject of this book will already possess a reasonable background knowledge of the mountain landscape and its wildlife. Nevertheless, before embarking on the Highland Round, it is important to prepare properly and to consider the few vital practicalities outlined below.

CLOTHING AND EQUIPMENT

Committing yourself to 13 or 14 consecutive days of walking means it is obviously necessary to carry a few more items of equipment than would normally be considered adequate in a day sack. The list below is the absolute minimum requirement of clothing and equipment, given normal late spring to late autumn conditions, when three- or four-season walking boots should be worn.

- Waterproof bag liner (a thick dustbin liner is ideal)
- Breathable waterproof outershell (cagoule and trousers)
- Fleece or jumper
- 3 T-shirts
- 3 pairs of socks
- Spare trousers
- Maps (see page 20 for sheet numbers)
- Compass
- Whistle
- Food and water (at least enough for one day)
- Basic first aid kit
- Warm hat and sun hat
- Sun cream
- Money (including credit cards and/ or cheque book)
- Identification
- Watch
- Head torch
- Knife
- Bivvy (survival) bag
- Toiletries
- Sunglasses
- Insect repellent (June–September)

Those embarking on the Round at other times, when there is significant snow on the tops, should wear four-season boots capable of accepting 12-point crampons and should also add the following to the contents of their rucksacks:

- ❖ **Ice axe**
- ❖ **Crampons**
- ❖ **Thermals**
- ❖ **Balaclava**
- ❖ **Emergency food rations**
- ❖ **Waterproof thermal gloves or mitts**

A rucksack with a volume of about 45 litres should be adequate for carrying the above items. Winter walkers or those choosing to carry a few extra items, such as binoculars and identification guides or, in the case of keen photographers, camera, lenses and filters, might consider going up to a 50-litre sack. My personal preference is for compression straps over exterior pockets, an arrangement that helps to keep the sack narrow on the back and allows for adjustments to its bulk as items are inserted or removed.

ACCOMMODATION

Appendix 1 lists selected bed and breakfast (B&B) type and hostel accommodation for each of the overnight stays. Although the list is by no means exhaustive for larger villages, in other places the accommodation shown may be all that is available. Where accommodation is limited, it may be necessary to arrange taxi or post-bus connections to find alternatives in other locations. More detailed references are included in the relevant sections where this could be necessary. Where choice exists, however, the selection shown has been made with those walkers on a limited budget in mind.

To take advantage of the cheapest accommodation, which is available at five locations on the Highland Round, the £6 annual membership of the Scottish Youth Hostel Association is money well spent. Prices at all hostels are standardized according to the grade of hostel and include bedding and a comfortable bunk. A nominal charge is made for hiring an inner sheet. Breakfast is not included but is usually available locally.

Hostels are particularly appropriate for walkers. The proprietors of some guest houses may, understandably, be averse to wet and muddy walkers entering their homes but hostels have designated washing and drying areas. Staying in youth hostels provides good opportunities to meet other lovers of the outdoors, to exchange experiences and to share grudges about the authors of walking guides, but they are never private places. In male dormitories at least, on a bad night, the 'snore' factor can render you an insomniac!

A final word on planning accommodation: even in peak season, try to resist the temptation of booking far in advance. If you are too committed, you will lose flexibility. Any delays resulting from unforeseen circumstances – atrocious weather, for instance, or blistered feet – could jeopardize your forward timings. A more pragmatic plan is to make arrangements up to two or three days ahead.

SAFETY

In general, the Scottish Highlands present tougher challenges for the walker than do mountains south of the border. Rugged, untamed terrain, remoteness, long distances, steep ascents, navigational problems and unpredictable weather are among the factors that conspire to render the high-level stages of this Round serious undertakings, even in summer. In winter they are mostly the preserve of experienced mountaineers, some sections becoming roped expeditions, with an array of additional problems and dangers, not least the problem of fewer daylight hours to complete a stage. In winter – from October to March – it would be prudent for all but the most competent on snow and ice to avoid the longer stages over the higher mountains by taking the low-level options instead.

Apart from the Country Code, which should be respected wherever you are, observe the Mountain Code for Scotland, as published on Ordnance Survey Outdoor Leisure Maps:

Before you go
- Learn the use of map and compass
- Know the weather signs and local forecast
- Plan within your capabilities
- Know simple first aid and the symptoms of exposure
- Know the mountain distress signals (see below)
- Know the Country Code

When you go
- If possible, avoid going alone
- Leave written word of your route and report your return
- Take windproofs, waterproofs, woollens and survival bag
- Take map, compass, whistle, torch and food
- Wear climbing boots
- Keep alert all day

If there is snow on the hills
- Always have an ice axe for each person
- Learn to recognize dangerous snow slopes
- Carry a climbing rope and know the correct use of rope and ice axe

If you need the rescue services, dial 999 and ask for the police. Follow the instructions you receive.

Mountain distress signals

The mountain distress signals are six long whistle blasts or torch flashes, repeated at one-minute intervals. If you do not have a torch or a whistle, you should signal in the same way with repeated shouts. Continue to repeat the distress signals until your rescuers are with you. The recognized answer is three whistle blasts or torch flashes.

NUTRITION

It has to be said that the Scottish Highlands are not known for their cuisine, and in most hotels the menu is unimaginative. Evening bar meals are normally a variation on the standard breaded haddock, chips and peas, while vegetarians on a prolonged visit to the region will find themselves overdosing on eggs and cheese.

Walking is hungry and thirsty work. While you are walking the Highland Round you will find that the most efficient way to maintain energy levels is to eat little and often. Eating great quantities in one go can actually have the opposite effect of diminishing your energy level. Apart from a good supply of sandwiches, consume fresh fruit, dried fruit, muesli bars or mint cake for quick energy boosts as well as drinking plenty of liquid to avoid dehydration.

CLIMATE

There is a saying in Scotland: 'If you do not like a particular season, wait an hour and another one will come along.' Nowhere in the country does this seem more apt than when referring to the Highland climate, and, as the cliché reminds us, one can experience all four seasons in a single day.

Anyone who reads only Tourist Board brochures before visiting the Highlands might be forgiven for thinking the hills enjoy a near-Mediterranean climate. The reality is very different, however, and it would be dangerous for walkers not to be properly prepared for adverse weather conditions.

The Scottish Highlands have higher rainfall levels than most of the United Kingdom, and the area as a whole is similar to the Lake District, although precipitation levels can vary greatly across the region. In the Western Highlands and across the area covered by this book, the weather is notoriously unpredictable and localized, but recent years have seen some kind of weather pattern emerging, with the months of May and September offering a good proportion of dry sunny days.

When you need a weather forecast for the region, tune in to the Outdoor Activities Forecast, which is broadcast by Radio Scotland (MW810khz/FM 92.4–97.7Mhz) each evening at 6.57pm (6.27pm at weekends), a free and usually accurate weather information service. Details of specific interest to walkers and climbers are given, including expected cloud-base levels, precipitation, windspeeds and temperature at 914m (3,000ft).

If you have committed a specific time to the Highland Round, you will obviously be at the mercy of the weather rather than having the luxury to pick and choose your days for walking. However, knowing what conditions to expect can help you plan with the alternative routes in mind.

A final word of warning to summer visitors: always carry insect repellent as a defence against *culicoides impunctatus* (the Highland midge), which is on the wing between June and September and often in ferocious swarms.

ACCESS

While the Criminal Justice and Public Order Act 1994 can in many ways be interpreted as a means of oppression, it is unlikely to affect walkers *de facto* freedom to roam, despite the now criminal offence of aggravated trespass. That said, walkers should nonetheless be alert to any misuse of the new law by landowners, although at the same time they should respect estate needs. With the exception of a few unsympathetic landowners, most are helpful in offering alternative routes away from the rifles during the stalking season.

Reflecting the urgent need for co-operation between different users of hill land, the pamphlet *Scotland's Hills and Mountains: a Concordat on Access* sets out the responsibilities and rights on all sides. Signed by the representatives of ten diverse groups early in 1996, it reflects a spectrum of concern and agreement, from the Scottish Landowners' Federation to the Mountaineering Council of Scotland, and it is an important step forward.

Forestry privatization remains a cause of some concern with regard to future access for walkers, but on the land that remains in the ownership of the Forestry Commission, there is often an excellent network of tracks and paths. The same is true on those National Nature Reserves that are under the auspices of Scottish Natural Heritage.

Deerstalking and other estate activities

Whatever your views, deerstalking provides income for Highland estates. The season normally begins in mid-August and, with the culling of hinds, can last until early February, although precise times may vary from estate to estate. Always consult locally.

Within the area covered by this book, restrictions during the deerstalking season are most likely to be imposed at the Auchessan Estate near Crianlarich, in the vicinity of Ben Starav in Glen Etive, at Carn Gorm on the north side of Glen Lyon and at the South

Chesthill Estate on the approach to the Lawers range. No such restrictions apply on National Trust for Scotland land.

The grouse-shooting season is from 12 August until 10 December, and similar restrictions on access to land may apply to protect this activity. Between March and May it is important to avoid disturbing sheep during lambing.

MUNROS

'Munro collecting' has reached obsessive proportions, and for a growing number of walkers in the Highlands, climbing Munros is a main objective of a day spent in the hills.

A Munro is simply defined as a separate mountain over 914m (3,000ft), but there continues to be much heated dispute as to what this actually means. Sir Hugh Munro listed 283 such mountains in 1891, but since then the list has been amended. Today, the Scottish Mountaineering Club recognizes 284 such summits.

This Highland Round, by way of the principal route outlined in the main text, traverses a total of 17 Munros. 'Collectors' can bag others by pursuing the optional route on Ben Nevis (Stage 7a) as well as high-level alternatives and extensions elsewhere.

Using this Book

The Highland Round is a 13-stage, long-distance, circular route, each stage representing one day of walking. To cover the very best of the mountains, lochs and glens of the Southern and Central Highlands, the route is a combination of high-level and low-level walking. For the purpose of this book, the term low level is used to define a stage where all walking is below 610m (2,000ft); high level defines a stage that involves a significant traverse on mountains above this height.

With the exception of the first three days, which are all high level, the stages of the main route alternate between high level and low level. This not only allows for variety in the type of walking involved, but also gives the walker an easier time on the days between the strenuous exertions of mountain climbing. The Highland Round is, by any standards, a tough and challenging route, linking together eight high-level and five low-level linear routes, not including optional Stage 7a.

A low-level alternative is given for each high-level stage, and, similarly, on a low-level day a high-level option is possible. In this way a degree of flexibility is achieved, allowing walkers to tailor the route as ability, inclination or the weather may dictate. In theory, it is possible to undertake the entire Round as a low-level route or, in the case of the exceptionally fit, to pursue the whole circuit as a high-level expedition.

Also outlined are suggestions for 'escapes' and 'extensions', which offer further alternatives to the main route. A summary at the beginning of the route chapters offers an overview of each stage.

Because of its strategic position and accessibility, Crianlarich is the starting and finishing point for the Highland Round. The village lies at the junction of the A85 and the A82, the main road arteries into this part of the Highlands. Perhaps more significantly, it has a railway station on the West Highland Line, is well served by the coach companies and is barely 1½ hours out of Glasgow. Because it is circuitous in nature, one could just as easily begin the Round at any other convenient point on the route, such as Tyndrum, Killin or Fort William.

The total distance covered is 265.4km (164.9 miles), which means a daily average of 20.4km (12.7 miles). The shortest stage, crossing Bidean nam Bian, is 11.6km (7.1 miles), while the greatest distance covered in any day is between Glen Nevis and Loch Ossian, a distance of 29.8km (18.5 miles). Total height climbed during the two weeks is 11,800m (38,704ft), which is greater than the height of Mount Everest! The traverse on the Ben Lawers range provides the greatest challenge in terms of height gained in a single day, being 1,650m (5,412ft). All these figures exclude Stage 7A, the Ben Nevis option.

MAPS

The outline map provided for each stage is marked with relevant place names and features. Relief cross-sections give the rise and fall along each stage. These cross-sections indicate where the climbs appear and how steep they are.

ABBREVIATIONS

To avoid constant repetition, a limited number of abbreviations have been used in the route description:

B&B	bed and breakfast	**NW**	northwest
E	east	**OS**	Ordnance Survey
ENE	east-northeast	**OSLR**	Ordnance Survey Landranger map
ESE	east-southeast	**S**	south
FC	Forestry Commission	**SE**	southeast
ft	foot/feet	**SNH**	Scottish Natural Heritage
GR	grid reference	**SSE**	south-southeast
k-gate	kissing-gate	**SSSI**	Site of Special Scientific Interest
km	kilometre/s	**SSW**	south-southwest
m	metre/s	**SW**	southwest
N	north	**W**	west
NE	northeast	**WHW**	West Highland Way
NNE	north-northeast	**WNW**	west-northwest
NNW	north-northwest	**WSW**	west-southwest
NTS	National Trust for Scotland	**YH**	youth hostel

GENERAL GLOSSARY

andesite	*brown-coloured igneous rock formed by rapid cooling of magma*
arête	*sharp mountain ridge*
bothy	*cottage or hut*
burn	*stream or brook*
Corbett	*individual mountain over 760m (2,500ft)*
croft	*small farmstead*
free-ranging	*traversing pathless terrain*
granite	*coarse-grained, pale, igneous rock formed by slow cooling of magma*
hag	*cutting in a peat bog*
Jacobite	*supporter of Bonnie Prince Charlie*
kirk	*church*
Munro	*individual mountain over 914m (3,000ft)*
quartzite	*pale, silica-based rock*
schist	*light-coloured, finely banded metamorphic rock*
shieling	*mountain hut used by shepherds*
spate	*river or stream in flood condition*

GLOSSARY OF GAELIC NAMES

Most Highland names for features and mountains are Gaelic in origin. In recent years there has been a revival of interest in the language, and today more Gaelic is being written and spoken than at any time since the Gaels first came from Ireland 1,500 years ago. Most of us, however, are confronted by an array of unpronounceable mountains, rivers and glens when perusing OS maps of the region, although attempts at a greater understanding can add to the pleasure of walking in Scotland. The words most often encountered and their English meaning are given here:

aber	*mouth of loch, river*	beg, beag	*small*
abhainn	*river*	ben, beinn	*hill*
allt	*stream*	bhuidhe	*yellow*
aonach	*ridge*	bidean	*pinnacle*
auch, ach	*field*	blar	*plain*
bal, bail	*town, homestead*	bothy	*hut*
ban	*white, fair, pale*	brae, braigh	*upper slope, steepening*
bealach	*hill pass*	breac	*speckled*

cam	*crooked*	glias, glas	*grey*
cairn	*pile of stones, often marking a summit*	gorm	*blue, green*
		inch, inis	*island, meadow by river*
carn	*cairn-shaped hill*	inver, inbhir	*confluence*
caol	*strait (kyle)*	lag, laggan	*hollow*
ceann, kin, ken	*head*	larach	*old site*
		lairig	*broad pass*
ciche, cioch	*breast, breast-shaped hillside*	leac	*slab*
		liath	*grey*
cil, kil	*church, cell*	loch	*lake (diminutive, lochan)*
clach	*stone*	mam	*pass, rise*
cnoc	*hill, knoll*	maol	*bare or bald (normally refers to mountain top without vegetation)*
coille, killie	*wood*		
corrie, coire, choire	*mountain hollow*		
		meall	*mound*
creag, craig	*cliff, crag*	monadh	*upland*
dal, dail	*field, flat*	mór, móre	*big*
damh	*stag*	odhar, odhair	*dun-coloured*
druim, drum	*long ridge*	rhu, rubha	*point*
dubh, dhu	*black, dark*	riabhach	*brindled or striped*
dun	*hill fort*	ruadh	*red, brown*
eas	*waterfall*	sgor, sgurr	*pointed*
eilean	*island*	sneachd	*snow*
eilidh	*hind*	sron	*nose*
eun	*bird*	stob	*pointed*
fada	*long*	strath	*valley (wider than glen)*
fionn	*white*	tarmachan	*ptarmigan*
fraoch	*heather*	tarsuinn	*transverse, across*
gabhar, ghabhar, gobhar	*goat*	tom	*hillock (rounded)*
		torr	*hillock (more rugged)*
		tulloch, tullach	*knoll*
garbh	*rough*		
geal	*white*	uaine	*green, pallid*
glen, gleann	*narrow valley*	uisge	*water, river*

Where known, the most commonly accepted English meaning of a Gaelic name for any mountain ascended is given in brackets in the principal heights section of the concise summary for the relevant stage.

MISCELLANEOUS

Maps and compass

All of the high-level stages, as well as many of low-level stages, demand the accurate use of a map and compass. Highland landscapes are typically bereft of easily recognizable reference features, and mist and low cloud are normal conditions on the highest summits. OS maps are essential wherever you wander in the Scottish Highlands. The Landranger Series (1:50,000) is perfectly adequate, although some walkers prefer the greater detail of the Pathfinder series (1:25,000). Four Landranger maps (OSLR) are required for walking the Highland Round: sheets 41, 42, 50 and 51.

Unfortunately, despite their general excellence, OS maps abound in Gaelic misspellings. In such instances, the spelling that appears on the OSLRs has always been used in this book.

Many paths described in the route descriptions are not marked on OS maps; on these occasions, rely on the route descriptions.

Compass bearings

All compass bearings have been given to the nearest $22\frac{1}{2}°$ point – e.g., E, ESE, SE. This is normally considered sufficiently accurate for safety, although extreme caution should be exercised on misted-out summits.

Dynamics

Along most of the Highland Round, footpaths are rarely waymarked or surfaced in any way and there are few stiles. For the sake of the wilderness, it must be hoped that things will not change much in this respect, although in some places it can be expected that new paths will get worn in.

Few man-made features change more frequently than the erection, dismantling and re-routing of deer fencing. Where reference is made to deer fencing in the route descriptions, be prepared for potential anomalies in the location of fence-lines and the gates between them. Other unforeseen diversions may be caused by ongoing forestry work, such as felling and tree planting.

Freeing yourself from the encumbrance of carrying a tent, a sleeping bag and associated paraphernalia means that you must expect to pay the small price of a little roadside walking at the beginning and end of each day in order to gain access to accommodation. Campers, however, have the opportunity to reduce their tarmac mileage to an absolute minimum.

Grading

Each stage of the Highland Round, as well as the main alternative option for that stage, has been allocated a grade between 1 and 6. In this way, walkers can quickly assess the overall difficulty and use it as an aid in considering whether alternative routes would be more appropriate to individual requirements. This grading appears in the concise summary at the start of each route description and can be simply defined as follows:

1 – easy and undemanding physically, without route-finding problems

2 – generally straightforward navigation and undemanding physically

3 – quite demanding physically, with route-finding difficulties possible in bad weather

4 – demanding physically, with likely route-finding problems in bad weather

5 – very demanding physically, with the probability of route-finding difficulties

6 – arduous and extremely demanding physically, requiring navigational skill

Many factors were taken into consideration in the allocation of these grades, including terrain, steepness, distance covered, total height gained, seriousness in the event of injury or bad weather and potential navigational problems. Gradings are based on late spring, summer and autumn conditions – that is, without significant snow cover. All the low-level stages are between grades 1 and 4; the high-level stages are between 3 and 6.

Time allowances

Time allowances are included in the summary sections as well as in the main text. They are based on the author's own performance and include periods for rest and eating. For the first two or three days out on the Round, compare the estimations with your actual performance to see if any adjustments to your plans are necessary.

STAGE 1
(HIGH LEVEL)

CRIANLARICH TO TYNDRUM VIA BEN CHALLUM

MAP: OSLR 50

STARTING LOCATION
Crianlarich YH/Station GR 385251
Parking available at various locations in Crianlarich

OVERVIEW/INTEREST
Good 'warm-up' route for carrying a heavier than usual back-pack.
Includes a pleasant, scenically diverse ramble on the WHW in Strath Fillan and a long but easy-angled ascent to a Munro.
Under snow, the route is a good introduction to the Scottish mountains in winter.
Quite demanding physically, although easily adapted to suit individual fitness, ability and inclination.

FOOTPATHS
Unmistakably clear and well-worn paths and tracks on WHW.
Unpathed yet straightforward climb to Ben Challum.
Good waymarking on the WHW.

GRADING: 3; low-level option, 1.

TIME ALLOWANCE: 8¼ hours

DISTANCE: 19.5km (12 miles)

TOTAL HEIGHT GAINED: 1,150m (3,770ft)

PRINCIPAL HEIGHTS: Ben Challum (Malcolm's Hill) 1,025m (3,364ft)

CRIANLARICH TO TYNDRUM VIA BEN CHALLUM

CRIANLARICH YH TO KIRKTON FARM

(Allow 1¾ hours)

Leave the YH and walk under the railway at Crianlarich station via the subway leading to the A82. From the other side of the road, take the WHW heading W into the forest, a path well waymarked and well worn. The hills rising above the village on the eastern side, notably Ben More and Cruach Ardrain, are seen well from here. Higher up, at a ladder stile on the left, the path joins the WHW from Glen Falloch. The splendid view into the glen and of the surrounding hills justifies a brief pause before you continue W along the WHW.

Head up above tiny Bogle Glen, but then veer left on a course generally NW by an undulating path between the young pines of a plantation. Chances are you will meet other Wayfarers on Scotland's first designated long-distance footpath. The popularity of the WHW is proving to be far greater than initial expectations, so much so that it has become something of an M25 among footpaths but in Strath Fillan it nevertheless provides a very convenient starting point for the Highland Round. From the highest point of the WHW in Strath Fillan, at about 360m (1,181ft) above sea-level, the extensive grassy slopes of an immediate objective, Ben Challum, dominate the eastern boundary.

Continue downhill, and cross a footbridge in the wooded ravine cut by the Herive Burn. Further down and closer to the road again, the WHW becomes more like a rough track, but speedy progress is maintained. Where a sign points down to 'Ewich B&B', turn left, in accordance with a yellow arrow and on a path that leads above the bank of a burn. Walk under the right-hand arch of a railway

View to Ben Lui across Strath Fillan, from above Kirkton Farm.

OVERLEAF

23

STAGE 1

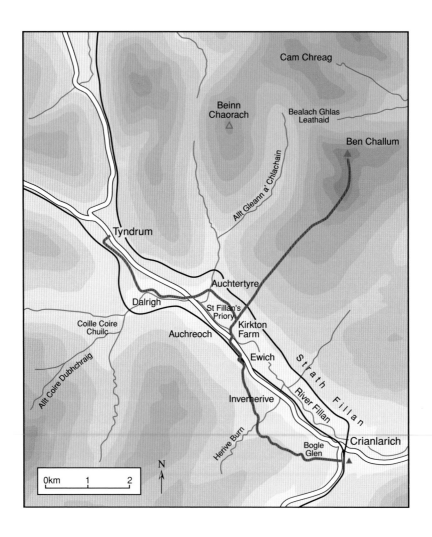

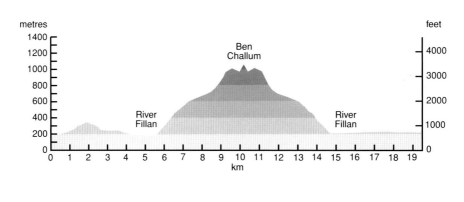

bridge and then bear left to cross the burn. From here, pick up a gravel path that soon leads up to the roadside. On the other side, walk NW along the top of a birch-strewn bank as far as a stile on the right. Go over it and out across a field to another stile, just before the sturdy timber bridge at the River Fillan. Proceed over that bridge to Kirkton Farm.

KIRKTON FARM
TO BEN CHALLUM AND BACK
(Allow 5¼ hours)

From the front of the farm bear left, passing between the remains of St Fillan's Priory and a graveyard on the right. St Fillan was one of the missionaries responsible for the spread of Christianity throughout the Highlands from the settlement of St Columba on Iona in AD563. The priory remains at Kirkton are thought to date from the fourteenth century.

After a cattle-grid, the WHW continues NW (see low-level option), but summit-bound walkers should instead pursue the track directly ahead. Pass to the right of a second graveyard and walk on up between a gap in a wall to cross the railway at an unofficial level crossing. There, leave the track and head NE on an unpathed but straightforward course up the grassy slope. Sheep fencing higher up should be crossed where it has been laid flat. Views back across the strath to Ben Lui, Ben More, Stob Binnein and Cruach Ardrain are perhaps the highlights of this ascent on an otherwise rather featureless hillside. With the emergence of Ben Challum and the surrounding hills to the N, at about the 600m (1,968ft) contour, comes more of interest. The gradient levels off here. Walk E, then ENE, on your way round between the heathery knolls of the high moor to come to the base of Ben Challum's southern ridge. Following a line of rusty fence posts up along the ridge should prove helpful in mist. Gradually swing N to reach the rocky knoll of the South Top. To gain the true summit, which lies ahead to the N, at first descend W, to walk around the top of a steep trench. If the summit is under snow, be sure to stay well away from the rim of the west-facing corrie. Descend in a dip before climbing the final 70m (230ft) to the summit cairn.

The best of the views are to the S and E, in the general direction of Ben Lui. Those to the N are partly obscured by loftier mountains such as Beinn Dorain. Returning by way of the ascent makes for a straightforward return over familiar ground and is certainly the recommended course in mist – follow the fence posts to come below the cloud-base.

Ben More, Stob Binnein and Cruach Ardrain from Ben Challum.

OVERLEAF

KIRKTON FARM TO TYNDRUM

(Allow 1¼ hours)

From St Fillan's Priory, take the WHW by the track leading NW beside the top of a plantation. After passing a cattle-grid located in the gap of a dry-stone wall, walk on to Auchtertyre Farm. On your right, behind a chalet, you will notice two wigwams, eco-friendly cabin accommodation for walkers built by the designer Charles Gulland. These high-tech structures are growing in popularity and are springing up all over the Highlands.

Beyond the Allt Gleann a' Chlachain, continue past the farm to the A82. Cross the road and take to a track beside the River Fillan, walking upstream to a junction with another track at the top of a bank beside a hump-back bridge. Continue W by a path and track on the north bank, a course through birch and plantation species, which is marked by the thistle signs of the WHW.

Leave the track for a less distinct path, which goes NW between the grassy hillocks above a stream on the right. On approaching Tyndrum, pass through a k-gate and begin a pleasant course weaving between Scots pines but in a wood lacking the biodiversity of the old Caledonian forest. Signs on fence posts advertise various B&Bs and hotels as well as a pack-carrying service (the latter is, alas, for those on the West Highland Way only). A bridge crossing the river on your right leads to Pine Trees Leisure Park, but instead, continue to the lane in front of Burnside Cottage. Turn right for Tyndrum, where the Tourist Information Office as well as various guest houses and hotels can be found.

ALTERNATIVE ROUTES

LOW-LEVEL OPTION
VIA THE WEST HIGHLAND WAY IN STRATH FILLAN
(Allow 3 hours)

The ascent of Ben Challum from Kirkton Farm is, in effect, tagged on to the WHW between Crianlarich and Tyndrum. Therefore, the obvious low-level option is to omit the climb on the mountain by not deviating out of Strath Fillan – that is, by following only the route outlined in the first and last sections of the description of the main route.

ESCAPES

Not unexpectedly, the fastest route between Crianlarich and Tyndrum is to follow the A82 all the way. Allow 2¼ hours. It is, however, a busy main road and following the WHW is preferable.

Those who would rather not climb a mountain on the first day but who would nevertheless welcome the opportunity of a little more exploring might consider wandering over to the rare remnant of old Caledonian forest at Coille Coire Chuilc. From the WHW, at Dalrigh, cross the hump-back bridge over the River Fillan and follow a rough track W, going over the railway. Further on, a bridge over the Allt Coire Dubhchraig gives access to the beautiful Scots pines. Allow up to 5 hours.

Those on a day trip can return to Crianlarich by a late train from Tyndrum.

EXTENSIONS

For most walkers committed to the Highland Round, the ramble through Strath Fillan and the climb up to Ben Challum are likely to prove sufficient for the first day. Remember, too, that carrying a heavier than usual rucksack might take a bit of getting used to. For these reasons, only an alternative way of descent from the mountain should be considered as a realistic means of extending the route.

From the summit, the obvious option is to drop down by way of the Ben's steep northwestern ridge to reach the Bealach Ghlas Leathaid. From here, the determined could, of course, climb Cam Chreag, going on even to Beinn Chaorach. Otherwise, descend Gleann a' Chlachain by following the stream to pick up a track that leads back down to the WHW at Auchtertyre. Allow an extra hour.

STAGE 2
(HIGH LEVEL)

TYNDRUM TO DALMALLY VIA BEN LUI

MAP: OSLR 50

STARTING LOCATION
Tyndrum, Strath Fillan GR330303
Parking available by Tourist Information hut

OVERVIEW/INTEREST
An exhilarating traverse on one of the most beautiful mountains in Scotland.
Ascent has a distinctive alpine character, via a corrie of historical significance.
Extensive views of the Southern Highlands, from two Munros.
Demanding physically, especially on ascent.

FOOTPATHS
Excellent Land Rover track on Ben Lui approach.
Faint path up the steep northeast rim of the Coire Gaothach.
Easy-to-follow path on a broad ridge connecting the two mountains.
Unpathed but straightforward descent from Beinn a' Chleibh, leading on to a good forest track.
Minimal waymarking.

GRADING: 4; low-level option, 3.

TIME ALLOWANCE: 8¼ hours

DISTANCE: 19.8km (12¼ miles)

TOTAL HEIGHT GAINED: 1,100m (3,610ft)

PRINCIPAL HEIGHTS: Ben Lui (Calf Mountain) 1,130m (3,707ft)
Beinn a' Chleibh (Hill of the Creel) 917m (3,010ft)

Tyndrum to Dalmally via Ben Lui

Tyndrum to Ben Lui

(Allow 3¾ hours)

Leave the A82 in Tyndrum by the road for 'Tyndrum Lower Station', beginning in front of the Ben Dorran Hotel. Cross the railway by the k-gates at the end of the road to pick up a forestry track heading S through the trees. Recently, gaps have opened up between the swathes of larch and spruce, the result of a forest fire in May 1994. Thankfully, the flames stayed N of the river, sparing the irreplaceable fragment of Old Caledonian Forest on the other side. As you look down Strath Fillan, Ben More and Stob Binnein dominate the skyline above Crianlarich.

Good progress is possible on the approach, so that the noise of traffic is quickly left behind. The track veers SW before heading down again and twisting left. Cross a stile over deer fencing and join the track that follows the River Cononish upstream, directly to Ben Lui. High up in the north-facing Coire Gaothach, clearly demarcated on both sides, snow can linger well into summer, giving a distinct alpine appearance on the approach. Less imposing are the grassy hill slopes on the opposite side of the river, culminating in Beinn Dubhchraig and Ben Oss (see Extensions). Grey wagtail and dipper sightings confirm the purity of the water, although the health of red foxes that patrol these banks is more at risk. Too frequently, poisoned meat is left out by farmers with lambs to protect. More enlightened shepherds realize that attempts to control numbers are usually futile.

From the mining access road on the right, 'Authorized Persons Only', walk on between the farmhouse and the new, bright green barns. On the left, a red arrow on a post indicates 'Route to Ben Lui this way', directing you away from the gold mine below Beinn Chuirn. After a metal gate the track rises above the river on a slightly steeper gradient. Beyond a second metal gate, drop down on the track, which terminates at the Allt an Rund, immediately below Ben Lui.

STAGE 2

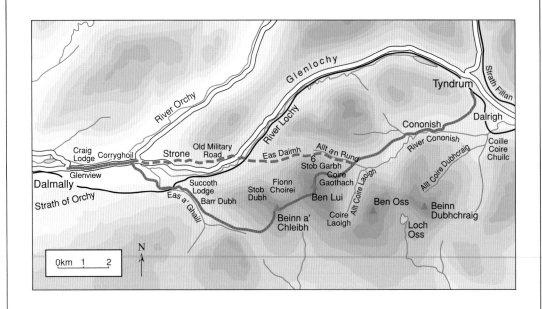

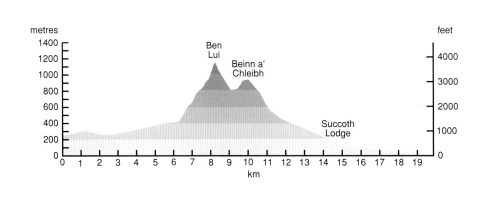

Do not be put off by the seemingly impregnable face of the mountain confronting you. The way to the summit from here is well within the means of the fit and capable hill-walker. Nevertheless, it is possible for those with less ambitious objectives to detour around the mountain via the pass on the northern side (see Low-level Option). Those committed to the climb, ford the stream and pass to the right of a ruined shieling. At first, walk up WSW by the path next to the obvious burn, tumbling from the corrie above. Stay above the right bank. In summer, plant enthusiasts can seek out rare alpine flora known to favour these slopes.

No problems other than steepness are likely to hinder progress on the way up into the Coire Gaothach, but pace yourself. It is wise not to race early on, only to collapse in a tired heap on a wind-chilled summit.

At the foot of the Coire Gaothach, leave the fading path and walk WNW over grassy mounds towards the projecting spur of Stob Garbh. A spring thaw may have deposited avalanche debris nearby. It is a place worthy of note, famous in mountaineering history as the corrie where Scottish winter climbing was pioneered in the 1890s but, unless you are a climber, do not attempt an ascent on the corrie headwall.

Having crossed a small burn, climb the steep slope leading up to the obvious ridge at Stob Garbh. Pick up the trace of a path up along the crest and ascend W over the sparser vegetation of schist slabs. Any protruding crags and outcrops can be avoided on the left side, although the short, easy scrambles over them can be fun.

Higher up, where the gradient eases, pause to take in the corrie scenery on your left. Out across a broadening horizon, the profiles of some noteworthy mountains can be clearly seen. Further on, the traces of paths to the left and right, suggest possible alternative routes. A tiny cairn marks the point at which the narrowing and steepening ridge bears SSW before the final push. Take care on shifting rock debris, where step-kicking may be appropriate to cross persisting snows. On reaching a cairn at the top, turn left and continue to the northwestern summit. A short walk SE along the ridge at the top of the corrie, over rocks visibly scratched and scoured by the crampon points of winter climbers, leads to the cairn on the true summit at 1,130m (3,707ft).

The rewards for the efforts of the climb of Ben Lui are commanding views of the Southern Highlands. There is the opportunity to preview future encounters on the Highland Round: the mountains of Argyll and Lochaber. Looking ESE across the Coire Laoigh, Ben Oss and Beinn Dubhchraig are Ben Lui's neighbouring peaks. Further S, the Arrochar Alps are prominent and Ben Nevis and Ben Cruachan can be seen among the more distant mountains between W and N on the compass.

BEN LUI TO SUCCOTH LODGE
(Allow 3 hours)

Retrace your footsteps for a few metres to return to the lowest point on the ridge between the two summit cairns. From there, turn left and then walk WSW towards the smooth, rounded top of Beinn a' Chleibh. A straightforward descent is made on a moderately angled slope, over some loose scree at first, via a twisting path down the broad ridge. In mist, follow a bearing of 250°. Looking back from lower down, Ben Lui appears distinctively less impressive from the south.

The lower of two cairns in the saddle marks the top of the path descending Fionn Choire on the right (see Escapes). However, without changing your bearings, ascend Beinn a' Chleibh on the clear path leading up from the col at 770m (2,526ft). At the top of the steep slope, where the ground levels out, continue beyond the first cairn there. The more obvious and larger summit cairn sitting on schist slabs, a little higher up, is reached after a stroll over the mossy ground at the southern edge of the plateau-like summit area. At 916m (3,007ft), Beinn a' Chleibh just qualifies as a Munro, but it is overshadowed in every way by Ben Lui. Nevertheless, it is a fine vantage point for admiring many of the mountains of the Southern Highlands.

Strike off S from the cairn to reach the edge of the summit plateau after about 100m (330ft). Then bear SSW and begin to walk down the grassy hill slopes heading towards the pylons below. Sweep around to the right as you descend, veering W and aiming for the top corner of the plantation. Having reached the perimeter fence line, follow it down SW to cross wet ground approaching the pylons. Pass through the large gate between the deer fencing on the right, when directly beneath the power lines. From here, follow the pylons through the forest gap on a spongy, wet, though mostly non-existent path. Follow a track down through the conifers on the left, immediately before the fourth pylon along. The track soon swings back around to the forest gap. From the small weather station beyond the fifth pylon, pick up the forest track off to the right.

Walk NW on a good, dry surface, enjoying the deciduous woodland in the vicinity of the Eas a' Chaill. The stands of birch and ash that adorn the bank sides are one of the loveliest aspects of the day. On emerging at an obvious clearing, climb over a stile next to a gate before passing between the cottages at Succoth Lodge.

Ben Lui from the River Cononish.

SUCCOTH LODGE TO DALMALLY
(Allow 1¹/₂ hours)

Take the left fork where the track divides in front of the white cottage. Continue W and, beyond a wooden gate after about 300m (1000ft), walk under the arch of a railway bridge above the right bank of the river. Pass to the left of Succoth Railway Cottages, the door of which is exquisitely adorned with painted flowers. From there, go over the timber bridge crossing the Eas a' Chaill. Pause at the shaded bank and immerse hot, aching feet in the cooling stream to give the necessary rejuvenation to complete Stage 2.

On the other side a track joins from the left, but bear right and continue down-stream, on the south bank. A forest track gives access to the main road after 1.8km (1¼ miles). Turn left and walk W, keeping to the wider verges on the right side of the often busy A85. On the way to Dalmally, the road stays close to the south bank of the River Orchy. Go past the police station – there are more B&Bs near the junction with the B8077.

ALTERNATIVE ROUTES
LOW-LEVEL OPTION VIA THE ALLT AN RUND AND THE EAS DAIMH
(Allow 5¹/₂ hours)

Use the Cononish approach to Ben Lui, as described in the main route. From the end of the track at the Allt an Rund, turn right and follow the burn upstream along either bank. On the north bank are a couple of ruined sheilings, but the rising ground on both sides of the river is characterized by wet, spongy and unpathed moor. However, no real difficulties will be encountered, and in spring and summer there is much of botanical interest to see.

Higher up, the Allt an Rund narrows to a mere trickle before petering out below the crags of Ciochan Beinn Laoigh. From here, the driest route is over the grassy hillocks of the undulating moor at the top of the pass.

On beginning the descent, the view across the Strath of Orchy reveals Ben Cruachan and Loch Awe. Walk W and aim for the lowest corner of the forest plantation in the dip below, following the course of a small stream that feeds the Eas Daimh. Beyond the gate in the perimeter fencing, pick up a wet path on the north bank. The ground underfoot is drier further down in the forest, and here the burn draining Fionn Choire joins forces with the Eas Daimh. At the bottom of the forest, cross the railway and then the River Lochy, which is shallow but invariably leaves you with wet boots if you do not take them off.

Cononish farm.

From the north bank, turn left and walk out to the main road. The Old Military Road begins off to the right, a few metres W along the A85. Follow the rough track W through the conifers – it is overgrown and is waterlogged in places – to regain the main road in Glenlochy at Strone after 3km (2 miles). Continue the hike W along the main road for 4km (2½ miles), finishing the day at the village of Dalmally, as described in the main route.

ESCAPES

From the end of the track on the Cononish approach, a longer route to the summit of Ben Lui, via the Coire Laoigh, avoids the difficulties of the rugged Coire Gaothach ascent. Follow the Allt Coire Laoigh up to the broad, grassy expanse at the head of the corrie, turn N and ascend the easy-angled southern ridge of Ben Lui to reach the summit.

The col between Ben Lui and Beinn a' Chleibh is the point of departure for walkers choosing to omit an ascent on the lower mountain. A cairn marks the top of a path that twists down the abrupt headwall of Fionn Choire. Lower down, walk NW to reach a stile at the forest perimeter and from there follow the path beside the burn that drains the corrie, located about 200m (650ft) W of the actual path marked on the OSLR map. After about 1.5km (1 mile), the burn converges with the Eas Daimh. From here the way to Dalmally is shared with the route described for the Low-level Option.

EXTENSIONS

Beinn Dubhchraig and Ben Oss can be included to make a longer traverse and a total of four Munros. From Tyndrum, walk SE along the WHW to Dalrigh in Strath Fillan, GR 341290. From there, cross the River Cononish and follow a track WSW to the Caledonian pine wood of Coille Coire Chuile. The ascent of Beinn Dubhchraig is best made by following the Allt Coire Dubhchraig SW, upstream, bearing S to reach the summit near the top of the grassy corrie.

Continue to Ben Oss by traversing the ridge encircling Loch Oss. A descent NW is followed by an ascent SW to reach the summit of the second Munro. From here, a broad descending ridge leads to the col at the top of the Coire Laoigh. The summit of Ben Lui is gained by the ascent of its straightforward southern ridge, although nothing can better the approach to this mountain than that via the Coire Gaothach. Allow an extra 2¼ hours.

Forestry track near Succoth Lodge.

STAGE 3
(HIGH LEVEL)

DALMALLY TO BRIDGE OF AWE VIA BEN CRUACHAN

MAP: OSLR 50

STARTING LOCATION
Dalmally, Strath of Orchy GR168273
Parking available at Dalmally kirk, Cruachan Power Station and other locations by A85

OVERVIEW/INTEREST
One of the classic high-level traverses of the Central Highlands.
A day of breathtaking mountain and seaward views.
Five separate summits over 914m (3,000ft), including two Munros.
Very demanding route – one of the toughest days on the Round.

FOOTPATHS
A pleasant rural lane through the Strath of Orchy.
Good track followed by unpathed ascent of the first summit.
Distinct path on narrow, boulder-strewn ridge above Coire Cruachan.
Steep, unpathed descent of grassy slopes.
No waymarking.

GRADING: 5; low-level option, 3.

TIME ALLOWANCE: 8½ hours

DISTANCE: 18.2km (11¼ miles)

TOTAL HEIGHT GAINED: 1,450m (4,760ft)

PRINCIPAL HEIGHTS
Ben Cruachan (Mountain of the Mounds) 1,126m (3,694ft)
Stob Dearg (Red Peak) 1,104m (3,622ft)
Drochaid Ghlas (Grey Bridge) 1,009m (3,310ft)
Stob Diamh (Stag Peak) 998m (3,274ft)
Stob Garbh (Rough Nose) 980m (3,215ft)

Dalmally to Bridge of Awe via Ben Cruachan

Dalmally to Stob Diamh

(Allow 3¾ hours)

Dalmally kirk (GR 168275) exhibits an unusual Italianate style and is well worth investigating before setting off. Built in 1810, it rises from a buttressed octagon design, and its distinctive white tower is particularly eye-catching. The roof timbers are said to incorporate that last remnants of the old pine forest of Glen Strae.

Leave Dalmally by the B8077 and cross the River Orchy at Dalmally Bridge. A few picture-postcard cottages are dotted among trees on the way to Stronmilchan, beside a road rarely frequented by traffic and from which there is a delightfully rural perspective on the Strath of Orchy. Views to the W are dominated by a high and curving ridge known as the Dalmally Horseshoe, your initial destination being one of these summits among a string of connected peaks.

The road turns in towards Glen Strae before returning to the A85 at a junction, 3.5km (2¼ miles) W of Dalmally as the buzzard flies. From here, it is possible to make out the ruins of Kilchurn Castle, lying 1km (⅔ mile) S on a promontory jutting out into Loch Awe. If you need a packed lunch or an early break, try the food and hospitality on offer at the Dreshaig Tearooms, just a little further down the road and overlooking the loch.

A metal farm gate is on the right, just before the road junction, giving access to a good track for commencing the ascent. Walk N at first – there is no significant gradient – curving below the slopes of Monadh Driseig. On veering NW, and later W, the track steepens on turning in towards the Horseshoe. Pass through a gate between sheep fencing, staying above the Allt Coire Chreachainn, and, where the track divides, take the left fork. Continue uphill, passing in front of what appears a disused quarry.

The ground becomes spongier and the track less distinct before a footbridge that

STAGE 3

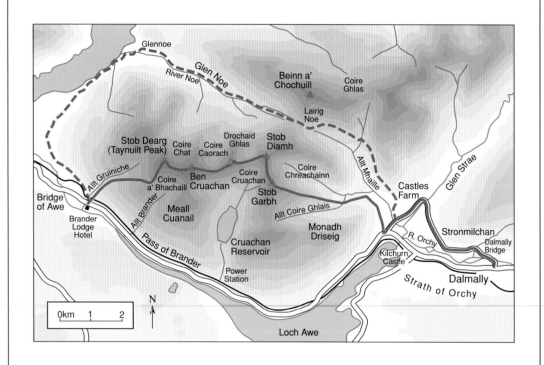

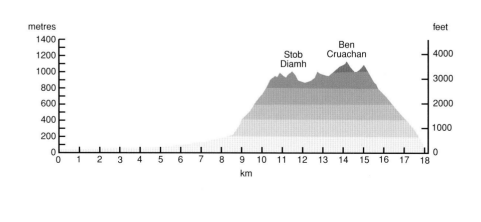

crosses the Allt Coire Ghlais. From the west bank, strike off WSW, aiming for the obvious grassy ridge rising up between Coire Ghlas and Coire Chreachainn. There then begins a seemingly endless plod up steep slopes heading WNW, levelling out only temporarily at about the 500m (1,640ft) contour. Above this point, the terrain is increasingly boulder strewn. It is an exposed place, where the nervous dartings of ring ouzels remind us that we are intruding on another's domain.

After a final push up onto the ridge leading to Stob Diamh, it is worth stopping at the cairn to catch your breath and to take in the new mountainscape. Of immediate interest is the wonderful horseshoe ridge surrounding Coire Cruachan. Exciting corrie scenery, magnificent peaks and truly memorable vistas are in store for those whose objective is Ben Cruachan.

Having raided your sandwich supply, walk N to Stob Diamh, passing over Stob Garbh on the way and pausing to admire the scenery around Coire Chreachainn. Stob Diamh is one of two Munros on this mountain range in miniature. On a northerly skyline, rising above the Glen Coe mountains, Ben Nevis dominates the mountainscape, while Scotland's longest stretch of fresh water, Loch Awe, extends as far as the southerly horizon.

STOB DIAMH TO BEN CRUACHAN
(Allow 2¼ hours)

The ridge continues for some distance, fulfilling the promise of a day of outstanding views. Leave the cairn by first descending W, following the obvious high-level path above a series of north-facing corries and leading eventually to Ben Cruachan. From the bottom of the first dip, ascend up along the rim of a corrie on your right. In places, the path traverses terrain that is arduous and rocky, although always immensely exhilarating.

Take care over the boulders on the slope before Drochaid Ghlas. The summit cairn is just a short walk out to the top of a rocky bluff on the right. The little extra effort required for this minor detour gives access to an unequalled vantage point. Looking W, Ben Cruachan and Stob Dearg appear as near-perfect cones, sharpened and sculptured by the glaciers that have here taken such deep bites out of their sides.

Return to the main spine of the ridge, turn right and continue W, descending easily over a series of outcrops for about 500m (⅓ mile). The hardest work of the day begins on scaling the Ben's rugged east-facing summit slope. As you approach the summit, a few of the moves between and over the granite boulders can be awkward and require some careful clambering. Stay well over to the right, close to the rim of the Coire Caorach. A broken triangular pillar now marks the highest point of the mountain.

Loch Etive, the long and beautiful finger of sea water that penetrates far into the mountain landscape of Argyll, points the way to Ben Nevis. Many of the mountain profiles in the N will now be familiar. Ben Lui and the Crianlarich hills lie to the E, but what makes Ben Cruachan unique among the viewpoints in this Highland Round is the opportunity to enjoy a seaward horizon. Across the Firth of Lorn is the Hebridean Island of Mull, the highest point of which is Ben More, the only island Munro outside Skye.

BEN CRUACHAN TO BRIDGE OF AWE
(Allow 2¹/₂ hours)

Perhaps because of its proximity to the western seaboard, Ben Cruachan is frequently engulfed by low cloud and has a reputation for sudden changes in weather. In such conditions, it is safer to descend on the southern side (see Escapes). Otherwise, continue on towards Stob Dearg, known locally as the Taynuilt Peak. A path across the ridge running W stays above Coire Chat, which is a little awkward coming down into the dip between the two peaks but is otherwise straightforward. A final and, at this stage, undoubtedly gruelling 100m (330ft) climb leads to the summit cairn on the Taynuilt Peak which offers yet finer views seaward.

Not included in the Munroists' itinerary and not normally included on most routes to its slightly higher neighbour, Stob Dearg is a largely undisturbed summit. On my last visit, it was a wonderful surprise to be startled by a succession of huge wings rising from behind the cairn: three eagles lifted off majestically and drifted out over Glen Noe. It was an exciting and unforgettable moment.

Leave the cairn and walk SSW, descending a mossy slope littered with boulders and staying close to the edge of the Coire a' Bhachaill. There is little evidence of a path, although sporadic cairns show the way to the col at GR 058300. At this point there is a large, moss-encrusted cairn, perched on a boulder overlooking the corrie. From here, walk out to the smaller one that lies about 80m (260ft) to the W, then continue downhill WNW. Go down the hill slope curving W, following the southernmost of tiny streams feeding the Allt Gruiniche. Mull is directly ahead on the horizon, although the upper limit of a forested area further down is a more convenient reference.

Next to the plantation, near the confluence of streams on the right, bear SW down a sheer hillside. Stay 50–80m (160–260ft) from the south bank of the Allt Gruiniche,

Kilchurn Castle, Loch Awe.

passing an impressive waterfall on the way down. Good grass cover allows for a safe descent, although the steep hill will punish tired knees. Cross some sheep fencing before gaining the trace of a path through the bracken.

Near the bottom of the hill, follow a fence line to pass through a wooden gate and bear left towards an obvious sheep enclosure. From here, go under the railway, turn right onto the road and cross the Allt Gruiniche. Try the B&Bs at Bridge of Awe or, alternatively, at Taynuilt 4km (2½ miles) further along the road.

ALTERNATIVE ROUTES
LOW-LEVEL OPTION VIA GLEN NOE
(Allow 7½ hours)

Obviously, a route that has its highest point at what is approximately half the altitude of Ben Cruachan will not be comparable in terms of panoramic views. However, this alternative route retains a wild remoteness along much of the way, venturing among mountains rather than on them.

Leave Dalmally by the B8077, following the road W as in the main route but departing from it earlier on. Follow an estate track off to the right, beginning about 800m (½ mile) before the junction with the A85. Pass in front of Castles Farm and climb the rising hill track NW, above the east bank of the Allt Mhaille. When you are near the top of the pass, leave the track and climb the last 100m (330ft) or so to reach the summit of the Lairig Noe at about 575m (1,887ft). Though effectively sandwiched between Beinn a' Chochuill to the N and Stob Diamh to the S, this exposed domain enjoys little protection from the westerly gales that blast through.

Continue NW, down into Glen Noe, following the flow of the numerous streams that feed the River Noe. Throughout the glen there are many interesting corners to explore among the debris of sheiling remains, as well as a few unusual viewpoints of the river tumbling over great rock slabs. Glen Noe once supported a sizeable community, notably the MacIntyres, a family believed to have come from the Western Isles, and led here by a white cow. The MacIntyres are said to have built their home where the cow lay down.

New fencing may dictate which bank of the river to walk by, before you emerge onto the lane beside a bungalow at Glennoe. Turn left, following a track beside Loch Etive to reach the valley of the River Awe, in reverse of the start of Stage 4.

Ben Cruachan from Drochaid Ghlas.

ESCAPES

It is a simple matter to walk by the busy A85 beside Loch Awe and on through the Pass of Brander if time is limited. Allow 4 ½ hours.

In adverse weather it is probably safer to descend from the summit of Ben Cruachan on the S side of the mountain. Go down across the boulder field to the col before Meall Cunail. From here two routes are possible: the one via the Coire a' Bhachaill and the Allt Brander on the W side, or the more frequented route via the Coire Dearg and Cruachan Reservoir to the east. There is a good track on the W side of Cruachan Reservoir. Further down, below the dam, a steep but well-used path leads to the main road near Cruachan Power Station (the starting point for day trippers with cars to return to). Of the two

View west from the Coire a' Bhachaill.

options, the pathless descent via the Allt Brander provides the fastest route to the road, with the further convenience of being that much closer to the Bridge of Awe. However, compared to the main route, this has little time advantage.

From anywhere near Stob Diamh, descend the ridge running S followed by the slopes that lead to the reservoir dam and the path to Cruachan Power Station. A walk by the A85 is then necessary to reach the Bridge of Awe. Allow up to 8 hours.

EXTENSIONS

For those prepared to endure well over 1,500m (5,000ft) of ascent for the day, begin the climb out of the Strath of Orchy on the east-facing slope of Monadh Driseig, walking on to Beinn a' Bhùiridh. From the second summit, drop down abruptly into the Lairig Torran, GR 096289, before continuing along the ridge rising N to Stob Diamh. Allow an extra hour.

Another alternative route to Stob Diamh from the E, and only marginally longer, is to ascend the ridge on the N side of the Coire Chreachainn.

No other suggestions for adding to this already long, hard day seem appropriate.

STAGE 4
(LOW LEVEL)

BRIDGE OF AWE TO GLEN ETIVE VIA LOCH ETIVE

MAP: OSLR 50

STARTING LOCATION
Junction with minor road to smokery, Bridge of Awe, GR 032298
Parking available at Bridge of Awe, Taynuilt and Inverawe Fisheries

OVERVIEW/INTEREST
A long walk of increasing mountain drama, beside a beautiful sea loch.
Encounters a series of delightfully wooded glens.
Opportunities for seal watching as well as for observing waders and sea birds.
A long and quite demanding route.

FOOTPATHS
Excellent, easy-to-follow lochside track on southern section.
Remote path that is awkward and wet in places north of Ardmaddy.
No waymarking.

GRADING: 3; high-level option, 5.

TIME ALLOWANCE: 8½ hours

DISTANCE: 25.9km (16 miles)

TOTAL HEIGHT GAINED: 150m (490ft)

PRINCIPAL HEIGHTS:
None. The highest point of the route is 80m (260ft) in the forest above
Inverawe at GR 032324.

BRIDGE OF AWE TO GLEN ETIVE VIA LOCH ETIVE

BRIDGE OF AWE TO GLENNOE

(Allow 2¼ hours)

Take the minor road leading off the A85 signposted 'Inverawe Fisheries and Smokery'. Go under the railway, turn NW and follow the lane through the trees above the east bank of the River Awe. Beyond a private road off to the left, continue N in the woods above the smokery. (Walkers beginning in Taynuilt, see Extensions.)

Leave the road at a forestry track on the right, passing a metal gate preventing access to unauthorized vehicles. After crossing the Alltan Dubh, take the left fork where the track divides. Where it divides the second time, turn right and head up a gently rising gradient through the conifers, away from Port na Mine. Below Barran Dubh the track surface deteriorates as you descend towards the loch. If you glance out to the open sea, the Island of Mull can be seen on the horizon.

After the coniferous of the earlier plantation forest, silver birch makes a welcome re-appearance on the steep slopes leading down to the loch shore. In spring primroses, bluebells, wood anemones and gorse blossom sparkle beneath the trees, painting splashes of colour on the environs of Loch Etive, which is without doubt one of the most beautiful lochs in Scotland. Continue down to meet the water at a lovely stretch of shoreline littered with seaweed-encrusted rocks. Veering right, follow the track beyond a row of larches to pass over a cattle grid before the bridge crossing the Allt Criche. Stay alongside a sandy beach for a while but then head away from the loch shore on the left. Further E, cross the River Noe at a sturdy timber bridge, a delightful spot for a picnic among the oaks and rowans of these attractively wooded banks.

STAGE 4

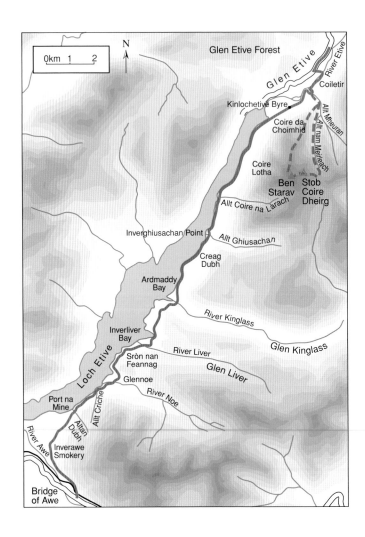

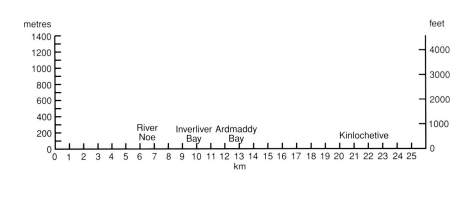

GLENNOE TO INVERGHIUSACHAN POINT
(Allow 2½ hours)

Once on the north bank, continue E, passing in front of the houses at Glennoe. From here, head back out towards the lochside and once there, about 40m (130ft) above the shoreline, turn NE. From the headland at Sròn nam Feannag, the view across Loch Etive promises dramatic peaks to the N but nearer to hand there is much birdlife to be observed, including waders and cormorants, and in the trees songbirds and cuckoos.

Use the footbridge to cross the River Liver before turning N. Beyond the farm buildings on the left, walk down to Inverliver Bay and then up over the higher ground. Dip down again to cross the River Kinglass. A bridge is located upstream of the river deposits that have created the interesting sandbanks in Ardmaddy Bay. For mountain scenery, look SE to Beinn a' Chochuill and the shapely top of Beinn Eunaich, the combined bulk of both dominating the high southern boundary of Glen Kinglass.

Soon after the red, white and black house, the last sign of habitation for some miles, the track gives way to a path less distinct than OS maps somewhat optimistically indicate. Progress from here on is somewhat slower. From the gorse scrub, walk NNE, close to the shoreline, staying almost at sea-level. At a solitary holly tree, boulder-hop to cross the first significant burn. Most intervening streams are not serious obstacles, but bog myrtle is evidence of the wet and awkward ground below Creag Dhubh. Keep an eye out on the left for seals, which can occasionally be seen wallowing in the more sheltered waters at the northern end of Loch Etive.

At Inverghiusachan Point pass the roofless shell of a cottage, and soon after the ruins of a settlement on the northern side of the Allt Ghiusachan.

INVERGHIUSACHAN POINT TO GLEN ETIVE FOREST
(Allow 3¾ hours)

Beyond Inverghiusachan, mountain slopes converge on Loch Etive to restrict the water to a narrower channel. Increasingly dramatic mountain scenery is coupled with a sense of remoteness and peace. For those who enjoy solitude, it is perhaps fortunate that few venture off the beaten track N of Glen Kinglass.

Close to where it enters the loch, cross the Allt Coire na Làrach, here little more than a trickle of water beneath a huge spread of boulders. The rocks seem to have spilled out from the corrie higher up, as if someone had emptied a tin of giant baked beans on the mountainside! Further N is a similar spillage of rocks from Coire Lotha. Here there is

some deciduous relief: a few birch trees enlivening the otherwise treeless domain below Ben Starav. Across the water is a very different topography exhibited by the Trilleachan Slabs, a sheer wall of pale strata and more sedimentary in character.

Beyond a shed walk ENE, away from the shoreline beside an inlet where, on the opposite bank nearby, there is a prominent copse of trees. Stay on the rough path skirting to the left of a grassy bank, again traversing spongy, wet moorland to reach a spread of rock debris, this time below the Coire da Choimhid.

From Kinlochetive Byre at GR 127455 (a Venture Scotland Bothy that is normally locked), keep to the path close to deer fencing and between gorse and alder scrub. Walk NE to cross the Allt Mheuran. Just before the footbridge, the great length and height of the ridge rising S to Ben Starav becomes apparent (see High-level Option). Also to the SSE, the pyramidal symmetry of Glas Bheinn Mhór is a splendid sight.

From the north bank, walk at first towards the confluence of the stream with the River Etive and follow the river upstream, passing the deserted cottage at Coileitir. Soon after, cross the bridge on the left and continue up, to join the road. Turn left and walk nearly 1.6km (1 mile) to the public telephone near Loch Etive House (see note at the end of this Stage). Unfortunately, there is no accommodation in Glen Etive.

ALTERNATIVE ROUTES
HIGH-LEVEL OPTION VIA BEN STARAV
(Allow 14 hours)

Although not easily integrated into the main route, there are one or two possible high-level options to satisfy those who never feel fulfilled until a mountain has been climbed. Ben Starav provides the most convenient candidate, although including this diversion to the main route is a formidable prospect at the end of an already long day.

Rising boldly above the northern shores of Loch Etive, the summit lies at 1,078m (3,536ft), every metre of which must be climbed. Begin at the footbridge over the Allt Mheuran and follow the path by the west bank before striking off S for the northern ridge, an arduous climb of unrelenting steepness. The speediest descent is to return the same way, although a more interesting way of return is to continue along the ridge running E. Some scrambling over granite blocks is necessary between the eastern top and Stob Coire Dheirg. From the col at 760m (2,500ft), turn down into the north-facing corrie

Loch Etive, near Glennoe.

Glas Bheinn Mhór from the Allt Mheuran.

to pick up a path on the western side of the Allt nam Meirleach. Continue downstream towards the River Etive to reach the footbridge from where the ascent began.

Ben Starav is a fine mountain in its own right and not deserving of the rushed approach. The traverse justifies a separate excursion.

ESCAPES

Although it is a long day, the route described is the most direct option for walkers venturing between Bridge of Awe or Taynuilt and Glen Etive. No curtailment is possible. The few scattered residences beside the track as far as Ardmaddy can, in theory, be called upon in emergencies, but the path N of Ardmaddy Bay is, however, unfrequented and remote, so make sure that you have informed others of your route intention, estimated time of arrival and so on, before you set out.

EXTENSIONS

To my mind the walk beside the east shore of Loch Etive is among the most rewarding, at least in terms of scenic beauty, of any in Scotland, and having reached Glen Etive you are sure to feel pleasantly tired and so extensions are not recommended, although determined walkers could pursue diversions into Glen Noe, Glen Liver or Glen Kinglass.

For those who spent the night at Taynuilt, begin Stage 4 by walking NE along the main road before picking up a path that crosses the River Awe at a suspension footbridge. The forestry track begins up in the trees to the E of Inverawe Fisheries and Smokery.

NOTE

As no accommodation exists in Glen Etive, on this occasion it will be necessary to telephone for a taxi to reach the King's House Hotel or the other B&Bs in Glencoe. There is a public telephone in Glen Etive at GR 127463. For the taxi service run by Alistair MacMillan, telephone (01855) 811460. To resume the Highland Round from Glen Etive for Stage 5, catch the post-bus back to the road near Coileitir the following morning (except Sundays) to continue the Round where you left it.

Ben Starav, from the River Etive at Coileitir.

OVERLEAF

STAGE 5
(HIGH LEVEL)

GLEN ETIVE TO GLEN COE VIA BIDEAN NAM BIAN

MAP: OSLRs 41 and 50

STARTING LOCATION
Glen Etive (Glenetive Forest near Coileitir), GR 137468

Parking at bottom of Gleann Fhaolain, on Glen Etive road near Dalness, GR 158509

OVERVIEW/INTEREST
An exhilarating ridge walk on the complex massif of Argyll's highest mountain.

Overlooks two of Scotland's 'showpiece' glens.

Fantastic views across Lochaber, the Central Highlands and beyond.

Day finishes at the 'Best Pub in Scotland' (CAMRA, 1994).

Very demanding physically; accurate compass work essential in mist.

FOOTPATHS
Some free-ranging necessary, up and down steep grassy slopes.

Rough path along the main ridge between summits.

No waymarking.

GRADING: 5; low-level option, 3.

TIME ALLOWANCE: 7½ hours

DISTANCE: 11.4km (7 miles)

TOTAL HEIGHT GAINED: 1,300m (4,265ft)

PRINCIPAL HEIGHTS:
Bidean nam Bian (Peak of the Mountains) 1,150m (3,772ft)

Stob Coire Sgreamhach (Peak of the Loathsome Corrie) 1,070m (3,510ft)

Glen Etive to Glen Coe via Bidean nam Bian

Glen Etive to Bidean nam Bian

(Allow 4¼ hours)

From Glenetive Forest follow the Glen Etive road NNE through the plantation area, reaching the Allt Fhaolain after about 5.3km (3¼ miles). Ahead of you note the U-shaped profile of the Lairig Gartain, a distinct glacial trough that separates the two Buachailles (shepherds).

Having crossed the bridge over the burn, where the road turns sharp right, head off to the left across a clearing in the trees on a faint path. A waterfall can be seen tumbling above the forest to the N. Walk upstream of the Allt Fhaolain, soon veering towards the main summit of Bidean nam Bian. Cross a ladder-stile over rusty deer fencing and turn right, following the fencing NE. Some ducking under spruce branches may be necessary to reach the bottom of the waterfall. From here head N across much steeper ground, on the western side of the burn and up towards the waterfall. The climb, while quite gruelling, is free of problems and occasional pauses can be recommended, not only to catch your breath but to admire the views of Ben Starav and Loch Etive.

An obvious outcrop by the waterfall at the top of the plantation is best bypassed on the left side. Cross a ladder-stile over rusty fencing. Veer NW away from the waterfall again, skirting to the left of further outcrops. Beyond them, resume an uphill course N. In spring bluebells and other wild flowers splash the steep, grassy hillside with colour, but later in the year they are swamped by a pervasive growth of bracken.

Pass to the right of a large rowan-covered outcrop where, to the E and looking beyond the top of the waterfall, a more extensive view of Glen Etive is possible. Walk NW for 200m (650ft) to reach a broad ridge running N above the burn which is in the ravine on your right. The gradient eases, but a path continues

STAGE 5

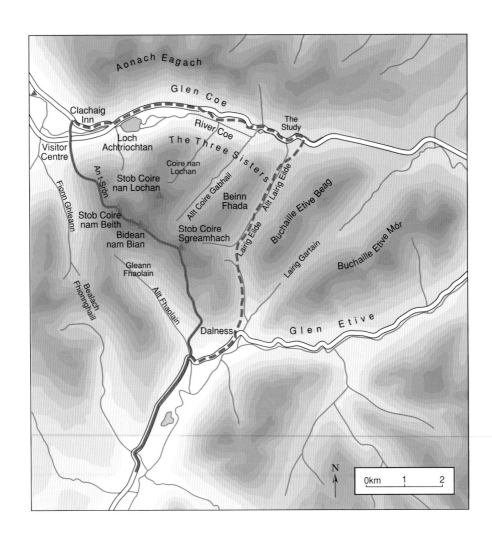

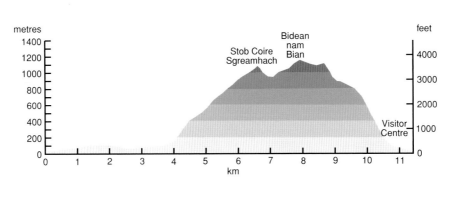

steadily uphill. Veer N over grass and rocks, coming close to an edge on your left that overlooks Gleann Fhaolain. Bidean nam Bian is an invigorating place in early summer: pockets of snow linger in the shady hollows between new green grasses and orchids, while slopes close to the the summit are a playground for energetic mountain hares.

At an altitude of about 800m (2,625ft), on slopes littered with boulders, the Buchailles emerge on the skyline to your right. At about 850m (2,788ft), there is an opportunity to top up water bottles from a last tiny burn. Veer slightly to the right and, where the gradient relents again, cross a more extensive scree field near the top.

The summit of Stob Corie Sgreamhach, a Munro marked by a small cairn, is especially memorable for the view it affords of so many mountains. The scenery is tremendous in all directions from this sanctuary high above glens on both sides, although the most famous of them all, Glen Coe, is mostly hidden by The Three Sisters. More prominent is the sensational Aonach Eagach ridge, beyond which rise the fabulous Mamore hills.

The name Bidean nam Bian refers both to the highest summit as well as the mountain as a whole. The main summit is close at hand and accessible by a traverse along the ridge heading NW. Another ridge extends NE from the summit, connecting with Stob Coire nan Lochan – an unparalleled display of beautiful mountain scenery.

Walk W from the cairn on Stob Coire Sgreamhach to reach a second cairn a few metres away, and then bear WNW. Care should be exercised when heading down steeply across the boulders. A cairn is reached at the bottom before the next steep ascent to the summit begins along one of two parallel paths heading NW. Near the top some boulder clambering is necessary before passing one or two further cairns, and from here the path leads up to the summit proper. At 1,150m (3,773ft) it is the highest point in Argyll. The now familiar sight of the Lochaber Mountains to the N are tantalizingly close, as are the other Glen Coe mountains, including the Buachaille Etive Beag and the Buachaille Etive Mòr to the E. Beyond Beinn a' Bheithir to the W lie Loch Linnhe and the sea. Many more mountains can be identified in the distance and in all directions.

BIDEAN NAM BIAN TO GLEN COE YH
(Allow 2¾ hours)

Leave the summit, heading W to reach a cairn on another top. Soon after, turn NW then

Looking SW down Glen Etive, from above Dalness.

OVERLEAF

N down a slope before the short climb up to Stob Coire nam Beith. From the vantage point of this summit, one may ponder on the rock and cliff scenery encircling the Coire nam Beith. Double back a few metres, bear right and walk out to a small cairn, before descending W on a steepening path down a scree slope. On veering NW again and staying near to the rim of the corrie, the ridge narrows on coming above Fionn Ghleann to your left. You must concentrate as you negotiate these rocks. The gradient eases as you continue N to the end of the ridge above An t-Sròn, from where the cliffs below Bidean nam Bian are perhaps seen at their best.

From here, a direct descent WNW down the steep hillside begins. There is something of a path at first over the rocks, but you must decide for yourself on the best route down the grassy slopes thereafter. The vegetation offers good grip on a route that gradually curves steeply N towards the NTS Visitor Centre.

As you reach lower levels, you are welcomed by bird song from among the scattered rowans and, sadly, by traffic noise too. At flatter ground, close to the road, pass the remains of a sheiling and walk over a ladder-stile. Cross the road and go over a second stile, walking behind the Visitor Centre and crossing the footbridge over the River Coe. Concrete steps lead up the opposite bank to a k-gate. From here, follow the path off to the right between the trees, signposted 'An Torr and Clachaig Hotel'. The path emerges at the roadside, just N of the Clachaig Inn. Turn right for refreshments and accommodation at the inn (voted 'Best Pub in Scotland' by Camra in 1994) or turn left and follow the road for 1.5km (1 mile) NW to Glen Coe YH.

ALTERNATIVE ROUTES
LOW-LEVEL OPTION VIA THE LAIRIG EILDE
(Allow 5¾ hours)

In terms of total mileage, this option covers a greater distance than the main route. However, as expected, significantly less ascent is involved and the route is relatively straightforward, mostly following distinct pathways.

The Lairig Eilde (Pass of the Hinds) is significant historically in that it was once frequented by the MacDonalds. At the N end one has a fine view of Glen Coe. From where the main route leaves the Glen Etive road, continue on to Dalness. Opposite the grounds of the house, take the path heading quite steeply N, above the left side of a burn. Higher up, cross the burn near its source. Soon afterwards, a large cairn marks the summit of the Lairig Eilde.

Continue by descending gradually through the pass. The path is distinct and simply follows the Allt Lairig Eilde downstream between the Buachaille Etive Beag and Beinn Fhada (the most easterly of The Three Sisters), to emerge in Glen Coe near The Study. From here, follow the path and road W, amid scenes of high drama to reach the Clachaig Inn (the reverse of the first 6km (4 miles) or so of Stage 6).

ESCAPES

The fastest route between Glen Etive and the Clachaig Inn is via Gleann Fhaolain (The Roadman's Glen), going over the pass at about 700m (2,300ft) before dropping down into Fionn Ghleann and walking out N. Allow 5½ hours. A way via the Bealach Fhionnghaill is a further possibility.

From the summit, the least time-consuming route is the one I have described, via the Visitor Centre to the inn and the road. This is also likely to prove somewhat less treacherous than descending any of the corries mentioned in the Extensions. From Stob Coire Sgreamhach, heading down the steep headwall of the Coire Gobhail offers probably the quickest descent to the road for help in emergencies.

EXTENSIONS

Venturing into the glens between The Three Sisters can be very rewarding. These routes are probably better regarded as approaches to Bidean nam Bian than as descent options. That said, however, as ways off the mountain, they offer slightly longer routes to the Clachaig Inn and the YH via Glen Coe.

Most interesting of all is the Coire Gabhail (the Lost Valley). Leave the mountain either from the ridge connecting with Stob Coire nan Lochan or from the one between the main summit and Stob Coire Sgreamhaich. In both cases, a steep descent via the corrie wall is necessary to reach the path leading NE out across the floor of the valley. Once at the bottom, cross over the River Coe by means of a footbridge and soon after head W along the path and roadside through Glen Coe to reach the inn or the YH. Allow an extra 1¼ hours.

Alternatively, and with a similar time allocation, walk out to Stob Coire nan Lochan and then down one of the two connecting ridges at the head of the Coire nan Lochan. Further down, pick up the path descending the corrie and later cross the River Coe

Bidean nam Bian, Stob Coire nan Lochan and the view beyond.

OVERLEAF

Stob Coire nam Beith from Loch Achtriochtan, Glen Coe.

by a footbridge. From there, pick up the path which leads W through the glen, as described above.

A final corrie alternative is to leave the ridge 500m (1,640ft) WNW of Stob Coire nam Beith. Care is needed at first on steep slopes of shifting scree, but the path leading out of the corrie, to Loch Achtriochtan, passes numerous waterfalls in some spectacular settings. Allow an extra 30 minutes.

Those walkers who prefer exploring at high levels can strike out NE from Stob Coire Sgreamhach or Bidean nam Bian on a choice of connecting ridges and peaks, later returning to the main spine of the mountain.

STAGE 6
(LOW LEVEL)

GLEN COE TO KINLOCHLEVEN VIA THE DEVIL'S STAIRCASE

MAP: OSLR 41

STARTING LOCATION
Clachaig Inn, Glencoe GR 128568
Parking available at NT Visitors Centre and lay-bys in Glen Coe

OVERVIEW/INTEREST
Brooding scenes of exceptional mountain drama in Scotland's most famous glen.
Outstanding views to Ben Nevis and the Mamores from the Devil's Staircase.
Quite demanding physically, although navigational errors are unlikely.

FOOTPATHS
Wet and indistinct in places in Glen Coe.
Straightforward but well-trodden and eroded on the WHW.
Good track approaching Kinlochleven.
Waymarking on the WHW.

GRADING: 3; high-level option, 6.

TIME ALLOWANCE: 6½ hours

DISTANCE: 17.8km (11 miles)

TOTAL HEIGHT GAINED: 500m (1,640ft)

PRINCIPAL HEIGHTS
Top of the Devil's Staircase 563m (1,850ft)

Glen Coe to Kinlochleven via the Devil's Staircase

Clachaig Inn to The Study

(Allow 2 hours)

The atmosphere of solemnity that prevails in Glen Coe affects most of those that visit this Glen of Weeping. Memories of 1692 serve only to exaggerate the oppressive shadows cast by the glen's high enclosing mountains.

From the Clachaig Inn, make your way along the road to the junction with the A82 by Loch Achtriochtan. A few metres before the main road, clamber up a cutting in a bank on the left and walk along the path NNE for about 100m (330ft). Turn right and walk across grass to pick up a faint path running parallel to the A82 to avoid the traffic. Extensive bracken may make this difficult in summer, in which case follow the road E. One or two of the pinnacles on the Aonach Eagach may be visible, high above on the left side, although its serrated profile and the magnificence of its traverse are not best appreciated from the glen. Prominent on the right side is a dark gash in the cliffs of Aonach Dubh (Ossian's Cave).

After a lay-by on the left, pick up the course of a more distinct path, which leads to a copse of trees before returning to the road again at Achtriochtan. When you are about 300m (1000ft) beyond the farm, walk down to a gate on the right and pursue a path running closer to the River Coe, now on the southside of the road but continuing E. From where the path passes below two lay-bys, go through a second gate. Seen over your right shoulder, briefly revealed between two of the Sisters, is the impressive peak of Stob Coire nan Lochan. A footbridge, lower down on the right, gives access to the corrie of the same name. Further E another footbridge connects with the path leading into the Coire Gobhail (the Lost Valley; see Extensions). From above the second bridge, bear left and go up to meet the road at Allt-na-reigh.

From the cottage at Allt-na-reigh, walk E by the roadside at first, but then

STAGE 6

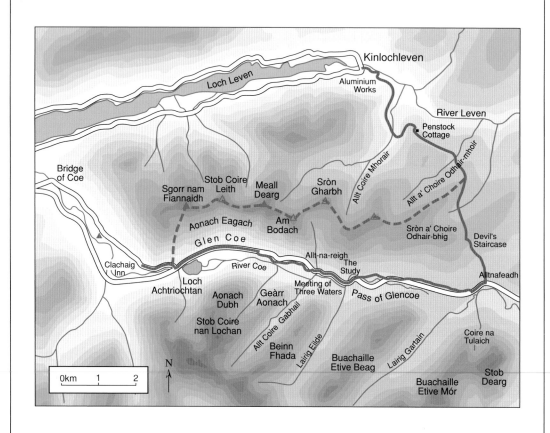

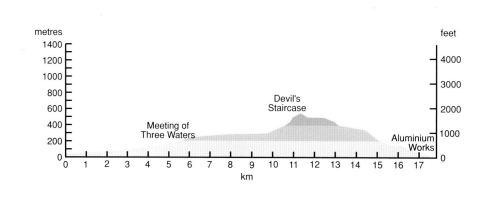

head up a bank on the left and follow a path beside a dry-stone wall. At a large cairn a little higher up take stock of the full drama of Glen Coe. From The Study, the buttresses of Beinn Fhada, Gearr Aonach and Aonach Dubh, known collectively as the Three Sisters, assume a spectacular prominence on the glen's abrupt southern boundary.

THE STUDY TO THE DEVIL'S STAIRCASE
(Allow 2¼ hours)

Stay on the track heading E, passing over a couple of hump-backed bridges. Note the large cairn by the road below, on the right, marking the bottom of the Lairig Eilde (see Low-level Option, Stage 5). Beyond the Pass of Glencoe, the glen broadens below the Buachaille Etive Beag.

Cross the main road where the track ends and continue by a rough path on the south side for about 250m (800ft). Cross the road again to resume a course on the N side, by a better defined, if wet, path, and from where the profiles of both the Shepherds of Etive emerge. Of the two, the Buachaille Etive Mór (Great Shepherd of Etive) is the bolder and less approachable mountain, while the Buachaille Etive Beag has a less complex massif. After about 2km (1¼ miles) the path ends at the roadside once more. From here, walk NE, either up on the grassy bank on the left or next to the traffic at the roadside, to reach Altnafeadh. Looking back, the valley of the Lairig Gartain is a beautifully smooth glacial curve – aesthetic perfection on a day already full of topographical wonders.

From a lay-by just before the small plantation area, strike off N away from the road along a rising path, signposted 'Public Footpath to Kinlochleven by Devil's Staircase'. This is also the WHW and consequently very eroded. Rudimentary footbridges make easy work of crossing streams on the way up over the heather.

On bearing NW, the path traverses increasingly steeper terrain while beginning to zigzag up the hillside. Stay to the left wherever the path forks. After a short, stiff climb the ground levels out towards a cairn at the top. Although you will need to catch your breath here, the Staircase is not the hell its name suggests and is certainly undeserving of its fearful reputation among West Highland Wayers. The association with the Devil recognizes the misfortune that befell the navvies who built the dam at Blackwater Reservoir. It is said that they used to indulge in outrageous drinking sessions at the King's

Lochan na Fola and the Buachaille Etive Mór, Glen Coe.

OVERLEAF

House Hotel and, on their return to their beds at Blackwater in the early hours of the morning, they would collapse in drunken stupors and freeze to death on the Staircase.

At the top, two cairns denote the summit of the pass, which, at 563m (1,850ft), is the highest point on Stage 6. There is also no loftier place on the WHW. To the N and S the views are quite magnificent. Stob Dearg, the Munro summit of the Buachaille Etive Mór, has a commanding presence. However, the tragedies that occurred in February 1995, when two separate groups of three climbers perished – all six were avalanche victims – within ten days of each other, while ascending the snow-filled Coire na Tulaich, should serve as an important reminder to all who doubt the seriousness of the Scottish mountains in winter. But it is to the mountains of Lochaber that we now look in excited trepidation. The Mamore peaks, backed by Ben Nevis, are strung out across a northern skyline in now tempting and close proximity.

THE DEVIL'S STAIRCASE TO KINLOCHLEVEN

(Allow 2¼ hours)

Leave the cairn and walk N on the unmistakable path, descending along the back of a broad corrie. After fording the Allt a' Choire Odhair-bhig, walk up again and pass to the right of a small ruin. Beyond the crossing of a second burn, bear right and keep to a rising gradient, before continuing downhill, more steeply, on a zigzag path NW. Cross the Allt a' Choire Odhair-mhoir at the footbridge and go on down to Penstock Cottage. Here, next to the water pipes that service the Aluminium Works, walkers are invited to register an opinion regarding proposed tearooms.

The thistle symbols of the WHW direct you down the good track that twists S through the trees. Cross the Allt Coire Mhorair at a concrete bridge at the bottom. A number of signs thereafter advertise guest house, bunkhouse and hotel accommodation in Kinlochleven.

Turn N again and walk back towards the River Leven and the lower section of the water pipes, beside which a final descent WNW leads to a wooden bridge on the right. Cross to the other side of the pipes and then follow a yellow arrow on a WHW post pointing along the road on the left, between the River Leven and the Aluminium Works.

When you emerge at the B863 in Kinlochleven you will find numerous B&Bs and other types of accommodation. A wide selection of these, together with a map of the village, appears on an information board on the N side of the bridge over the river. A somewhat smaller selection is given in Appendix 1.

ALTERNATIVE ROUTES
HIGH-LEVEL OPTION VIA THE AONACH EAGACH
(Allow 9 hours)

Looming high on the northern boundary of Glen Coe, the Aonach Eagach is rightly regarded as the most sensational ridge traverse on the Scottish mainland. Only those with well-practised scrambling skills, who relish the adrenaline rush of narrow airy pinnacles, should attempt the traverse. Described below is the way along the ridge from W to E, possibly involving even more difficulty than by the more frequented E to W traverse. Attempting the Aonach Eagach involves a serious commitment because there is no by-pass nor any viable escape route once you are on the ridge.

From the Clachaig Inn, walk along the road to the junction with the A82 near Loch Achtriochtan. Strike off on a path heading N, confronting the steep south face of Sgorr nam Fiannaidh direct, all the way to the summit. A longer, but distinctly more pleasant ascent, and one that is convenient for those staying at the YH, is possible via the Pap of Glencoe from the minor road at GR 111587. An easy-angled ridge rising SE connects the two mountains, from where there are fantastic seaward views across Loch Leven.

Sgorr nam Fiannaidh is a Munro, but the summit also marks the western extremity of the Aonach Eagach. Begin the traverse by walking E along a straightforward ridge to Stob Coire Leith. After a short but steep descent there begins some especially exciting scrambling over the first of a prolonged series of pinnacles, chimneys and rock slabs. 'Daunting', 'intimidating' and even 'despicable' are words that have been used to describe the Aonach Eagach traverse, and all may seem appropriate as slow progress is made to Meall Dearg. After an abrupt descent E from this summit at 953m (3,127ft), a final section of hard scrambling on 20m (66ft) of rock, leading up to Am Bodach, completes the traverse.

A path leaves the ridge on the Glen Coe side, from the col before Sròn Gharbh. For Kinlochleven, however, it is better to continue along the easy ridge E. Leave it by finally descending NE at Sròn a' Choire Odhair-bhig, to pick up the WHW, about 1.5km (1 mile) north of the Devil's Staircase.

Those who seek a high-level route but would rather not confront the Aonach Eagach can, of course, join the ridge at Sròn Gharb, having come up from Allt-na-reigh.

ESCAPES

A glance at the map shows that the easy route to Kinlochleven is by the B863. Slightly more interesting variations on this route are possible by using the network of Forestry

Commission colour-coded trails in the forest at Hospital Lochan. From the Bridge of Coe, walk N to gain access to the B road. A more adventurous route is possible by the path that goes NE, joining the road further E. Allow 3¾ hours.

These latter routes, or indeed any option that avoids Glen Coe, would seem to make little sense, however.

EXTENSIONS

The environs of Glen Coe are an outdoor lover's paradise. The possibilities for hillwalkers are endless, and exploring the area could occupy many pleasurable days or even weeks. A few convenient suggestions that are easily assimilated into the main route are outlined below, although devising your own would not be difficult.

The Lost Valley (see also Extensions from Stage 5) offers one of the finest possible corrie diversions. From the footbridge over the River Coe near Allt-na-reigh, use the path heading SW to explore the Coire Gobhail before returning.

Another option that ventures through two historic passes, both in the past used by the MacDonalds, involves a circuit around the Buachaille Etive Beag. First, follow the path SSW into the Lairig Eilde, beginning opposite the igloo-like cairn at GR 188563 (reversing the route outlined as the Low-level Option for Stage 5), and then, from Dalness, return via the Lairig Gartain. Allow an extra 4 hours.

There are many high-level options apart from the Aonach Eagach ridge traverse. One of the best is to the Buachaille Etive Mór, by way of the Coire na Tulaich. A path climbs the corrie direct from Altnafeadh. By returning from Stob Dearg the same way, the ascent becomes a convenient appendix to the main route. Allow an extra 3¾ hours.

Ben Nevis and the Mamores, from the top of the Devil's Staircase.

STAGE 7
(HIGH LEVEL)

KINLOCHLEVEN TO GLEN NEVIS VIA THE MAMORES

MAP: OSLR 41

STARTING LOCATION
Kinlochleven Aluminium Works GR 188619

Parking available in Kinlochleven

OVERVIEW/INTEREST
A traverse along the central spine of one of the finest mountain ranges in Scotland.

Passes through upland woodlands with much wildlife interest.

Includes two Munros (others within striking distance).

Outstanding and varied views lasting for much of the day, in the proximity of Britain's
highest mountain.

Physically very demanding route.

FOOTPATHS
Waymarked path and track initially.

Good stalkers' paths in the corries.

Mostly straightforward on ridge with some awkward clambering over loose rocks
on Am Bodach.

Tarmac lane (unfrequented by traffic) on final approach to YH.

Minimal waymarking.

GRADING: 5; low-level option, 3.

TIME ALLOWANCE: 8¼ hours

DISTANCE: 19.2km (12 miles)

TOTAL HEIGHT GAINED: 1,400m (4,590ft)

PRINCIPAL HEIGHTS
Stob Coire a' Chairn (Peak of the Corrie of Cairns) 981m (3,218ft)

Am Bodach (The Old Man) 1,032m (3,385ft)

Sgor an Iubhair (Peak of the Yew) 1,001m (3,284ft)

KINLOCHLEVEN TO GLEN NEVIS VIA THE MAMORES

KINLOCHLEVEN TO STOB COIRE A' CHAIRN

(Allow 3¼ hours)

Walk out to the N of the town, bearing W after the bridge over the Allt Coire na Ba. Opposite the school, take the path up into the trees on the right by signs for Mamore Lodge Hotel and the WHW to Fort William, walking behind a white bungalow. The woods are delightful, often alive with birds, including, in summer, willow warblers and spotted flycatchers, as well as dragonflies and butterflies. The gradient steadily steepens, but the path is well worn and easily followed NW. As height is gained, a few of the Glen Coe mountains are seen again through gaps in the trees to your left.

Where the path divides at a thistle symbol post, take the right fork, leaving the WHW and soon joining a tarmac track. From here, turn right and walk ENE. The occasional glance back reveals the true extent of the Aluminium Works and the water systems feeding it, while a little further on the sight of one or two of the Mamore peaks heralds a return to the mountains.

After the lane twists left, pass in front of the Mamore Lodge Hotel and then bear right, heading NE on the unsurfaced road. Follow the footpath sign that directs walkers around to the right of the white, slate-roofed houses. Walk on below birch scrub and veer N on nearing the Allt Coire na Ba. On reaching the foot-bridge, cross the river to the east side, taking the left-hand track at the fork towards sheep pens.

Continue upstream on the stalkers' path, heading N into the grassy corrie encircled by three of the Mamore Munros, two of which will be climbed later. Intervening burns, easily crossed, provide final opportunities to replenish water bottles before the real hard work. Tumbling down from Am Bodach on your left,

STAGE 7

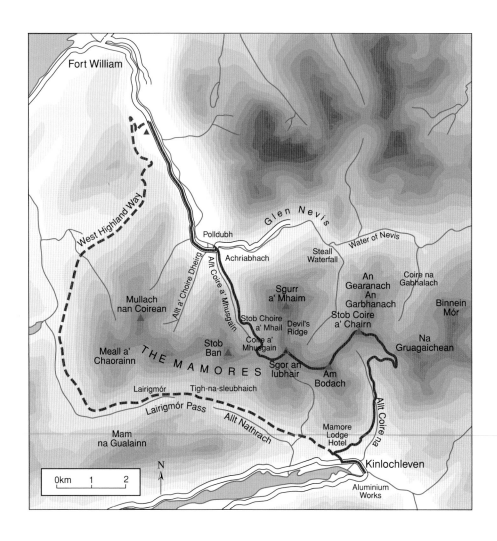

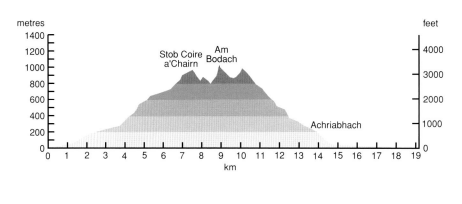

a waterfall nourishes a seemingly misplaced ribbon of birches, sheep-proof in an inaccessible ravine on a mountainside otherwise bereft of trees. After passing a prominent cairn, the going is wetter for a while. The path twists to the E, and the gradient steepens appreciably up the grassy slopes below Na Gruagaichean. On veering SE, the climb eases where the path twists up past a peaty pool on the left at GR 197651. At a small cairn, veer sharp left on a hairpin bend, turning away from a less defined path that continues S. A few untidy cairns mark out the climb northwards, until a final steep push leads on to the main spine of the Mamore ridge, below Na Gruagaichean.

A well-deserved rest allows quiet contemplation of the peaks encircling Allt Coire na Gabhalach at the eastern part of the range. Easily identified among them is the distinctive, wedge-shaped top of Binnein Mór, the highest of them all. The Mamore Hills are characterized by pale quartzite summit rocks, which give a permanent snow-capped appearance to many. Follow the unmistakable ridge path leading NW up over grass to the rocky top of Stob Coire a' Chairn. It is a Munro affording a superb outlook on the mountains to the N across Glen Nevis. Crowning them all, of course, is the huge bulk of Ben Nevis. A long, narrow arête connects the Ben with the red top of Carn Mór Dearg (see Stage 7a), while further E rise the magnificent Aonachs and Grey Corrie peaks. The Glen Coe mountains and ridges seem less foreboding from here, while the Mamore peaks, N and W, exhibit some of the many splendid features of this unique range.

STOB COIRE A' CHAIRN TO SGOR AN IUBHAIR

(Allow 1¾ hours)

From the cairn, walk W across the top and then head SW down a narrowing grassy ridge. Having first gone over a small rise, an arduous 200m (656ft) of ascent follows. An eroded path twists up a steep and rocky slope; great care is required clambering over easily dislodged boulders. The difficulty in reaching Am Bodach is rewarded by perhaps the finest view of the day from the highest point of the route, at 1,032m (3,385ft). Situated more or less in the centre of the range, the other Mamore peaks effectively span out from it along an array of connecting ridges projecting W, N and E. Among features of geological interest are what appear to be strata beds in many of the outcrops, which is surprising, given that these rocks have undergone a long history of metamorphosis.

On Am Bodach there are three cairns, marking three separate viewpoints. To continue the traverse along the central spine of the ridge, follow the path downhill and W to reach the col before the final summit of the day. An easy climb over the quartzite rubble preludes the last of the mountain top views at the large cairn on Sgor an Iubhair. From there, the most challenging and exciting part of the range is accessible: the narrow and airy arête known as the Devil's Ridge (see Extensions).

SGOR AN IUBHAIR TO GLEN NEVIS YH
(Allow 3¼ hours)

Continue the traverse by beginning the descent SW over boulder-strewn, mossy terrain, staying well away from the top of the sheer cliffs on the right. Veer W lower down and where to your right the great bulk of Sgurr a' Mhaim can be better observed. The Lairig-mor Pass and the WHW (see Low-level Option) are seen looking down to the S.

Near the lowest point on the ridge, before Stob Ban, turn off to the right and pursue the path that descends the upper reaches of the corrie. Thereafter, a good stalkers' path provides the obvious route through the Coire a' Mhusgain. Ford the upper reaches of the Allt of the same name and follow it downstream, on its E side, below the impressive east-facing cliffs of Stob Bàn. Further on, turn W for a while and head steeply down a series of zigzags, coming closer to the stream again. Ignore a path off to the left and instead continue through the birchwoods that adorn the lower reaches of the corrie. Peregrine falcons are often seen and heard in the vicinity, a happy reminder that these birds at least are now on the increase throughout Scotland.

Near the bottom, the ground is appreciably wetter before becoming a track that leads to a stile. From the road near the bridge over the River Nevis at Polldubh, turn left for a pleasant stroll along the lane and beside the river and meadows of lower Glen Nevis. The YH is a further 4km (2½ miles) towards Fort William. A forest walk above the road offers an alternative finish to the day.

ALTERNATIVE ROUTES
LOW-LEVEL OPTION VIA THE LAIRIGMOR PASS
(Allow 6½ hours)

Take the path out of Kinlochleven described in the main route, but do not leave the WHW where it divides. Follow the waymarked path to join the track W of the Mamore Lodge Hotel and there turn left. On the way up there are one or two excellent viewpoints over Loch Leven, towards the Pap of Glencoe.

The Glen Coe mountains from the Devil's Ridge.

Walk W on a level, well-drained track that was once Caulfield's Military Road but which now services armies of walkers on the WHW, battling on to its terminus in Glen Nevis. Stay above the north bank of the Allt Nathrach to reach the rather unspectacular summit of the pass, near the house at Tigh-na-sleubhaich.

A mile further W is the sad ruin at Lairigmor, the broken walls of which can now only offer protection to walkers in bad weather. The mountain Mam na Gualainn dominates the south side of the glen here, while the westernmost peaks of the Mamore Hills demarcate the north side, their barren hill-slopes both restricting the course of the pass and limiting the view.

Continue on the track that skirts around Meall a' Chaorainn, entering the first of the plantation areas encountered on the descent northwards. At its north end, the WHW and the Military Road part company; from here, Caulfield's route is a single-track tarmac road and the Way is a rough path.

Stay on the WHW, heading NE, through swathes of sitka spruce further on, Ben Nevis beckoning at close quarters and dominating the view ahead. The path steepens near the bottom, before joining waymarked forestry tracks in Nevis Forest, from there on providing the luxury of an easy descent to Glen Nevis YH.

ESCAPES

Having gained the ridge and the summit of Stob Coire a' Chairn, the fastest, most direct route to Glen Nevis is via the ridge immediately N. Walk on and up to An Garbhanach and then over the Munro An Gearanach, before descending N. A step path makes for a punishing descent in the enclosed corrie, which leads down to the Water of Nevis. Pass in front of the Steall Waterfall to reach the cable foot-bridge by the Mountain Rescue Hut. There, cross the river for the path leading through the wooded gorge to reach the car park and the road out of the glen. For finishing at the YH, this route has only a marginal effect on the total time allocation. Allow 30 minutes less.

For a quicker route but one that still includes one major peak, continue NW above Kinlochleven to where the WHW is a track and walk on to the bottom of the corrie below Am Bodach. Climb the corrie by the path off to the left, at GR167632, to gain the ridge E of Sgor an Iubhair. Climb that summit for the view before making a descent via the stalkers' path in the Coire a' Mhusgain. Allow 1¾ hours less.

The most difficult part on the main route of this stage, the 200m (656ft) climb to Am Bodach, can be bypassed by a path to the N. Rejoin the ridge before an easy climb W leads up to Sgor an Iubhair. Allow 30 minutes less.

EXTENSIONS

From the main spine of the ridge across the Mamore Hills, there are many other routes to Glen Nevis. Peaks at either the west or east end of the range can be tagged on. Of the various options, the Devil's Ridge has to be one of the most exciting, many considering it the finest section of the entire range. The ridge connects Sgor an Iubhair and Sgurr a' Mhaim, making the traverse along its sharp crest a very convenient alternative for the adventurous.

At Sgor an Iubhair, turn N and head down across boulders to the col before Stob Choire a' Mhail. The initial climb is straightforward enough, but the ridge beyond narrows significantly. The path to Sgurr a' Mhaim is obvious, although some scrambling is necessary near the lowest point before the final summit is reached. Experienced climbers will judge the test an easy one, while those lacking a head for heights may consider the prospect a little daunting. Beyond the ridge, a simple climb on broader slopes leads up to the distinctive quartzite top of Sgurr a' Mhaim, another Munro summit.

From the cairn, head NW down an obvious shoulder, below the screes, on slopes which are sufficiently steep to demand care and concentration if twisted ankles are to be avoided. Near the bottom, pick up the path beside the Allt Coire a' Mhusgain, just S of Achriabhach. Allow an extra 45 minutes.

One of the finest viewpoints of and from the Mamore range can be enjoyed from Stob Bàn. For this alternative, walk W from Sgor an Iubhair and continue in that direction uphill, having reached the top of the stalkers' path in the Coire a' Mhusgain. It is possible to return to the stalkers' path (allow an extra hour) or, alternatively, walk on over the broad ridge leading to Mullach nan Coirean. To descend from this Munro, on the western edge of the range, leave the summit, heading in a generally NE direction. Follow a narrowing ridge to come above a forestry area. From there, keep to the path beside fencing and leading NW to a stile, just before a burn, at GR133682. A wet path gives access to a forestry track and Forest Walk at Achriabhach. Allow an extra 2 hours.

The traverse of all 10 Munros of the Mamores in a single day is certainly a considerable challenge, providing the very toughest·of tests for fitness, endurance and sheer bloody-mindedness. Allow all of a very long summer's day!

The Mamores, from Stob Bàn.

OVERLEAF

STAGE 7A
(HIGH LEVEL – OPTIONAL)

BEN NEVIS AND THE CARN MÓR DEARG ARÊTE

MAP: OSLR 41

STARTING LOCATION
Glen Nevis YH, GR 128718
Parking possible by YH or near Visitor Centre at Achintee

OVERVIEW/INTEREST
Unfrequented approach to Britain's highest mountain via a long, narrow arête.
Spectacular views from the extensive summit plateau with many features of interest.
Includes two Munros, both over 1,220m (4,000ft).
Competence and accuracy with map and compass essential.
Arduous and extremely demanding route.

FOOTPATHS
Seriously eroded on 'tourist route'; wet near Lochan Meall an t-Suidhe.
Unpathed on slopes below Carn Beag Dearg.
Rugged on exposed arête where worst of awkward sections can be bypassed.
Minimal waymarking.

GRADING: 6

TIME ALLOWANCE: 8½ hours

DISTANCE: 15.8km (9¾ miles)

TOTAL HEIGHT GAINED: 1,750m (5,740ft)

PRINCIPAL HEIGHTS
Carn Beag Dearg (Little Red Cairn) 1,010m (3,317ft)
Carn Dearg Meadhonach (Middle Red Cairn) 1,179m (3,868ft)
Carn Mór Dearg (Big Red Cairn) 1,220m (4,003ft)
Ben Nevis (possibly Venomous Mountain) 1,344m (4,410ft)

Ben Nevis and the Carn Mór Dearg Arête

Glen Nevis YH to Carn Beag Dearg

(Allow 3¾ hours)

Having completed Stage 7 and arrived at the foot of Ben Nevis, the compulsion to climb Britain's highest mountain before continuing on the Round is likely to prove irresistible. It is to accommodate such urges that this circuit is included, necessitating another day of walking and a further night spent in Glen Nevis or Fort William.

Opposite the YH, go over the footbridge at the River Nevis and then climb the well-engineered path ENE. It meets the track from Achintee Farm after about 800m (2,600ft). Here, bear right on the first of a series of hairpin bends as the 'tourist path', always busy with hillwalkers, twists uphill below Meall an t-Suidhe. Severe erosion is kept at bay by continual path repair and resurfacing, and there are foot-bridges over all the burns. It is impossible to get lost but do keep to the signs indicating the 'Ben Nevis Footpath'.

At about 600m (1,968ft) the gradient eases. Walk across spongier ground by the path leading NE to a cairn, from where the 'tourist path' continues S (see Escapes). Instead, turn left and walk N on a rough path above Lochan Meall an t-Suidhe. Intervening burns are forded easily as their waters spread out across the peaty moor. Ignore the first less distinct path off to the right, but at a second cairn since leaving the 'tourist route', bear NE and pass between a line of rusty fence posts to come above the Allt a' Mhuilinn.

From here, turn in to the Coire Leis and walk ESE towards the Allt a' Mhuilinn. At a huge split boulder, possibly the largest among many littering the slopes below Castle Ridge, leave the path by striking off to the left and down to cross the river by easy boulder-hopping. Pick up a good path up on the opposite bank, turn left and walk

Sgurr a' Mhaim from the SW slopes of Ben Nevis.

OVERLEAF

STAGE 7A

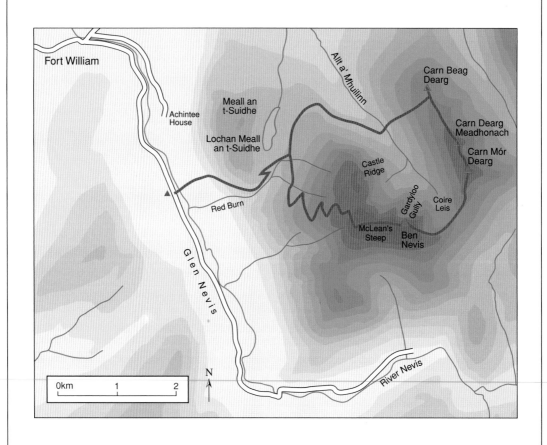

Fort William

Achintee House

Meall an t-Suidhe

Lochan Meall an t-Suidhe

Allt a' Mhuilinn

Carn Beag Dearg

Carn Dearg Meadhonach

Carn Mór Dearg

Castle Ridge

Gardyloo Gully

Coire Leis

Red Burn

McLean's Steep

Ben Nevis

Glen Nevis

River Nevis

0km 1 2

N

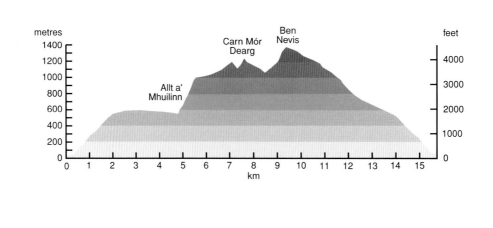

NW for about 300m (1000ft). Leave this path at a point that seems to give the least problematic course up the slope on the right, below Carn Beag Dearg.

Ascend NE up a steepening hillside, where playful mountain might may catch your eye as they dash between rocks. If possible, stay close to the more prominent of burns, which flows in the most visible of stony gullies. It is a gruelling climb over moss and boulders, with more than 450m (1,476ft) of height gained, but the view emerging to the S reveals an awe-inspiring array of cliffs, gullies and ridges.

Higher up, where the gradient eases, there exists the faint trace of an ascending path, but instead, walk E across scree towards a noticeable dip in the ridge profile. Having gained the ridge, turn left for a short stroll to the summit of Carn Beag Dearg. The outskirts of Fort William can be seen, but of more note is the view E, across the corrie of the Allt Daim. The ridge above the gondola run connects Aonach Mór and Aonach Beag, both in the mountain premier league of 'Scottish Fours' (mountains over 4,000ft).

CARN BEAG DEARG TO BEN NEVIS
(Allow 2¹⁄₄ hours)

Turn and walk SSE, continuing on a straightforward ascent over Carn Dearg Meadhonach. From here, a sparsely vegetated ridge, notable for the pink granite that gives this trio of peaks their names, leads up to the summit of Carn Mór Dearg. At over 1,220m (4,000ft), it is an incomparable vantage point for admiring the buttresses and cliffs of Ben Nevis.

From Carn Mór Dearg it is possible to assess something of the extent and difficulty of the narrow rocky crest that curves around the rim of the Coire Leis, the Carn Mór Dearg (CMD) Arête. Proceed S across the granite until, after 200m (650ft), the slopes fall away abruptly on both sides. The ridge sharpens to a narrow arête, and hopping and scrambling over the huge granite blocks of its crest makes for a thrilling traverse in the proximity of the impressive Northeast Buttress. A faint path just below on the southeastern side avoids the awkward bits and much of the exposure. The ridge curves SW before reaching its lowest point where a little further on it merges into the southeastern slopes of the Ben. At this point, there is an abseil post marking the top of a possible descent into the Coire Leis (see Escapes). It also marks the start of a final steep climb of more than 250m (820ft) up a bouldery slope, to reach the top.

Ben Nevis and the Carn Mór Dearg Arête.

OVERLEAF

The summit is at 1,344m (4,410ft) above sea-level and suddenly it seems that you have emerged into a different world. It is a vast 36ha (90 acre) boulder plateau, which, on a fine summer's day, is positively crowded. However, there is much of interest here, apart from a substantial cairn hosting the triangulation pillar. In fact, there is a large array of memorial cairns of all kinds, paying tribute to the victims of war or commemorating the casualties of the mountain. There is a prominent emergency shelter as well as the ruins of an observatory. Alas, it is also Britain's loftiest rubbish dump, with a shameful littering of tin cans, plastic bags, polystyrene, broken glass and just about everything else. When you stand on the roof of Britain, however, nothing can take away from the tremendous feeling of achievement. On a clear day your reward is a view apparently over all the Highlands. It is a prize you will no doubt have to share, but there is plenty to go around. There are mountains in almost every direction, and on a western horizon, far out to sea, some claim to have seen Northern Ireland! The mountains in the distance, as well as in the vicinity, and easily identifiable in clear weather, and include the Mamores, the Glen Coe mountains, Ben Cruachan, Ben Lui, the Cairngorms and, to the N and W, the Torridons, Kintail and the Cuillin of Skye.

BEN NEVIS TO GLEN NEVIS YH
(Allow 2½ hours)

Walk SW across the summit plateau from the triangulation pillar, keeping well away from the cliff edge. More walkers wander dangerously astray here than anywhere else on the mountain (see adverse weather recommendations on page 103). After 150m (490ft), turn right at the top of Gardyloo Gully and walk W to pick up the well-worn tourist path across the bouldery plateau. Once on the path, it is difficult to get lost. There are cairns to guide you over an otherwise quite featureless, almost quarry-like terrain.

A steeper descent begins with the first of an endless succession of zigzags, and those who savour the mountain will be grateful not to have suffered so on the way up. Loch Linnhe to the W and the Mamore peaks to the S do their best in providing a degree of interest on the way down. Eventually, the barren, rock-strewn slopes give way to a green carpet of rough grass.

After the last bend, cross Red Burn by a rough stone bridge before reaching the cairn where the path bears sharply left, returning to the point where you earlier deviated from it, close to Lochan Meall an t-Suidhe. Stay on the 'pony track' for the remainder of the descent, in reverse of the upward route.

ALTERNATIVE ROUTES

ESCAPES

Those who doubt their abilities on narrow ridges or are not prepared to commit to such a long traverse to reach the summit of Ben Nevis should use the 'tourist path', up and down. Allow 6 hours.

Climbing Ben Nevis is never anything less than a serious undertaking. In adverse weather a descent into the Coire Leis is possible from the abseil post on the edge of the corrie, at the end of the arête. However, if there is snow at the head of the corrie, an ice axe is essential. On no account attempt to descend the dangerously steep slopes on the southern side of the mountain. A steep descent W is also possible from Carn Mór Dearg. There are more fatalities each year on Ben Nevis than on any other mountain in Britain. The most common accidents happen to walkers who wander dangerously astray on the summit in mist. It is vital not to underestimate the potential hazards of a summit that is obscured by cloud nine days in every ten and which records an average mean temperature of just below freezing.

To descend from the summit, in adverse weather, follow the recommendations published by the Lochaber Mountain Rescue Team, outlined below:

1. From the summit trig. pillar walk 150m (490ft) on a grid bearing of 231° to near the top of Gardyloo Gully (first marker pole).

2. Then follow a grid bearing a 282° to clear the plateau. (A second marker pole is situated 300m (985ft) along this second bearing, at the top of McLean's Steep.)

Note: At present (1997), magnetic north lies about 5° west of grid north for Ben Nevis. In order to calculate magnetic bearings – i.e., the value you set on your compass – it is necessary to add 5° to these grid bearings. This adjustment will decrease by about 1° every six years.

EXTENSIONS

The circuit described achieves the main objective of prolonging the Highland Round: climbing Britain's highest mountain. Having gone the challenging way, by the mountain lovers' route, extensions are neither practical nor appropriate.

Nevis Forest from the 'tourist path' below Meall an t-Suidhe.

OVERLEAF

STAGE 8
(LOW LEVEL)

GLEN NEVIS TO LOCH OSSIAN VIA THE NEVIS GORGE

MAP: OSLR 41

STARTING LOCATION
Glen Nevis YH, GR 128718
Parking available at roadside in Glen Nevis for day trippers

OVERVIEW/INTEREST
Breathtaking scenery in one of the most beautiful Scottish glens, frequently described as 'Himalayan' in character.
A spectacular gorge set between the Mamore peaks and Britain's highest mountain.
A route of unfailing interest, including waterfalls, meadows, mountains, lochs, woods, and open moorlands.
A lengthy and physically demanding route.

FOOTPATHS
Begins on metalled lane.
Well-trodden path, rugged in places through gorge.
Often wet underfoot across grassy moorland.
Good tracks on approach to Loch Ossian.
Minimal waymarking.

GRADING: 4; low-level option, 5.

TIME ALLOWANCE: 10¼ hours

DISTANCE: 29.8km (18½ miles)

TOTAL HEIGHT GAINED: 600m (1,970ft)

PRINCIPAL HEIGHTS
None, highest point is at 370m (1,214ft).

GLEN NEVIS TO LOCH OSSIAN VIA THE NEVIS GORGE

GLEN NEVIS YH TO STEALL RUINS

(Allow 2¾ hours)

For staying at Loch Ossian or Corrour you should stock up with enough food for two days before setting off from Glen Nevis.

Superb scenery more than compensates for the narrow, 7km (4½-mile) strip of tarmac that penetrates one of Scotland's most beautiful glens. Apart from the summer season, the lane through Glen Nevis is rarely busy and allows for a good pace to be established early on.

At first, head S from the YH, in reverse of Stage 7, as far as the bridge at Polldubh. From here the final section of road is followed E, upstream of the River Nevis and beneath crags and cliffs popular with rock climbers. The road terminates at a car park below a prominent waterslide just to the N.

From the far end of the car park, pick up the path signposted 'Public Footpath to Corrour 15 and Rannoch 25'. The day finishes just beyond Corrour. Walk on above the north side of the Water of Nevis. The well-trodden path enters an attractive woodland of mixed tree species, including birch, rowan, pine and hazel. Where the path forks, stay left, taking the direction indicated by a yellow arrow. Cross the Allt Garbh at a footbridge, from where the path swings S.

Gaps in the trees on your left allow you to look back along the river to the W. The real excitement, however, is happening just below, where water forces a course through a labyrinth of channels and holes before bursting out in fierce cauldrons and rushing on. Closer scrutiny reveals that centuries of erosion have sculptured weird and sensual shapes in the bed rocks of the gorge.

As you approach the bankside, you are suddenly released from the confines of the Nevis Gorge. Out in the open, the lovely cascade of the Steall Waterfall

STAGE 8

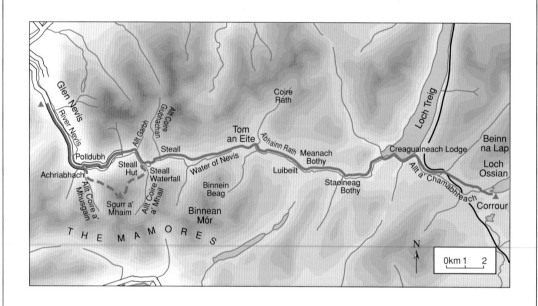

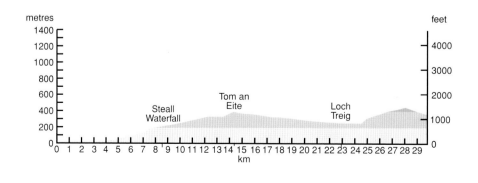

provides the perfect backdrop to a serene, grassy meadow, completing the overall picture of a glen that is frequently described as 'Himalayan' in character.

Keep to the path that skirts the edge of the meadow, ignoring a path off to the right that leads to the cable foot-bridge by Steall Hut. Bear left across the gravelly plateau formed by river deposits on the north bank. Pause here to admire the third highest water-fall in Britain and an especially fine example of a hanging valley. Continue ENE across ground that becomes increasingly wet underfoot and on to the sturdy foot-bridge over the Allt Coire Giubhsachan at the Steall ruins.

STEALL RUINS TO LOCH TREIG
(Allow 5¼ hours)

Of geological interest is the distinctive, almost sedimentary-like banding in the outcrops of schist that were seen on the Mamores ridge. Across the river is the rather detached con-ical peak of Binnein Beag, while glances back to the scene above Steall will help you to appreciate more fully the outstanding topography of the area. In Glen Nevis, both the aesthete and the academic will find much to occupy a prolonged stay, but there are many more miles to cover before darkness falls.

Beyond the ruins, continue E, following an undulating path that is a pale impression of quartzite in the grass. Take the left fork at a cairn 1km (⅔ mile) E of Steall ruins, rising gradually into a broadening glen. The small burns intervening from the left are insignifi-cant obstacles. Where the river twists south towards below Binnein Mór, keep walking E on a peaty, often wet path. The pale skeletal roots of pines from the ancient forest, as well as orchids and a varied upland flora, including devil's bit scabious, add botanical interest in what is a largely treeless moor.

Approaching the upper reaches of the Water of Nevis, pass to the right of a grassy bank at Tom an Eite. Having reached the head of Glen Nevis below the peaks of the Grey Corries, cross the stream that drains the Coire Rath at a convenient boulder-hopping point. This may require a short diversion upstream, before continuing downstream by the north bank of the Abhainn Rath.

From here, the landscape has an open, rather featureless character, which is punctu-ated only occasionally by a solitary rowan or birch. On the opposite bank, a coniferous

The River Nevis and the Mamores, from the foot-bridge by Glen Nevis YH.

OVERLEAF

copse of half a dozen or so trees highlights the ruined shell of a deserted cottage at Luibeilt.

Keep S of Meanach Bothy, and when you are beyond it, stay close to the river. At a series of waterfalls, the banksides become wooded, marking a return to a more confined valley. Follow a rugged path on an appreciable descent. Lower down, near a ruin on the opposite bank, pass Staoineag Bothy. Stepping stones lead across to it.

Pass through a tighter, more densely wooded ravine to reach a flat, grassy area, veering generally NE to reach Loch Treig. From a copse of Scots pines, cross the river by the bridge in front of Creaguaineach Lodge.

Loch Treig to Loch Ossian
(Allow 2¼ hours)

Follow the rough track, signposted 'Path to Rannoch', along the south shore of Loch Treig to cross a timber bridge over a burn after nearly 1.5km (1 mile). After the bridge further on, which crosses the Allt a' Chamabhreac near to a 'corrugated' hut, turn right and climb SSE on the track that rises away from the lochside. It then veers E and later forks. Take the path on the left, passing under the railway, beside another stream. Cross this about 70m (250ft) to the E of the railway using a rudimentary bridge. Pass in front of a ruin and walk ESE on the rising path that flanks the slope of Beinn na Lap, then head down towards Loch Ossian. Pick up the obvious track at the bottom, continuing E to reach the YH.

Alternative Routes
High-level Option via Sgurr a' Mhaim
(Allow 12¾ hours; main route + 2½ hours)

In this case, a wish to climb hills perhaps underestimates the considerable investment of energy that the direct route already demands. Nevertheless, the most practical high-level alternatives exist on the Mamores range, where the possibilities are almost limitless.

Within the vicinity of Glen Nevis, the ascent of Sgurr a' Mhaim offers a convenient diversion, but such a route has the unfortunate consequence of bypassing the spectacular Nevis Gorge. Leave the main route by the path from Achriabhach, heading up the east bank of the Allt Coire a' Mhusgain. After 500m (1,650ft), strike off up the NW shoulder,

Steall Waterfall.

climbing steeply to gain the pale rocks of the mountain's quartzite top. Sgurr a' Mhaim is an ideal point from which to admire Ben Nevis at close range, as well as the other 'Fours' on the north side of the glen. Leave the summit cairn by the northeastern ridge, eventually coming above the trees a few hundred metres W of the Allt Coire a' Mhail. From this point, great care is required as you descend through the dense woodland: a treacherously steep and slippery path leads N to the Mountain Rescue Hut. Cross the Water of Nevis by the swaying cable bridge to pick up the main route for continuing E.

A day of unrealistic ambitions is theoretically possible by incorporating Sgor an Iubhair and the Devil's Ridge (see Extensions, Stage 7).

Numerous other high-level options can be devised on the mountains above Glen Nevis. As with Sgurr a' Mhaim, such routes will inevitably be encountered early in the day, while limbs are still fresh. Remember that having coming down from the Mamores, plenty of mileage remains on the trek E to reach Loch Ossian.

ESCAPES

Although it is long and tiring, the route is nonetheless the most direct between Glen Nevis and Loch Ossian. Because there are no escapes, it involves a serious commitment.

EXTENSIONS

No extensions are recommended for Stage 8, which covers a greater distance than any other day on the Round. In the unlikely event that you feel restless on arriving at Loch Ossian, it is possible to circuit the loch on the track around it. Membership of the exclusive 'run around the loch in under the hour club' is for aspiring Olympians only! (Details are available at the YH.) Day visitors will need to plan around public transport timetables for connections between Glen Nevis, Fort William and Corrour. Catching an early train to Corrour and then pursing the route in reverse is possible.

NOTE

From Easter to the end of October, Gaelic Bus runs a service between Fort William station and Glen Nevis Youth Hostel. This service, four times a day, will be useful for day visitors (see Extensions) as well as for those having to stay overnight in town if the suggested accommodation in Glen Nevis is full.

Rowan at Beinn nan Each.

115

STAGE 9
(HIGH LEVEL)

LOCH OSSIAN TO BRIDGE OF GAUR VIA CARN DEARG

MAP: OSLRs 41 and 42

STARTING LOCATION
Loch Ossian YH, GR 371671

OVERVIEW/INTEREST
Route begins at an idyllic YH beside a remote loch.
Expansive views across a vast and desolate landscape from an easily attained Munro.
The day ends in the valley of a picturesque river.
Without difficulty, although quite demanding physically.

FOOTPATHS
Reasonable path rising above Loch Ossian.
Unpathed on Carn Dearg.
Good Land Rover track beside Allt Eigheach.
Finishes on an unfrequented road.
Minimal waymarking.

GRADING: 3; low-level option, 2.

TIME ALLOWANCE: 7½ hours

DISTANCE: 20.6km (12¾ miles)

TOTAL HEIGHT GAINED: 650m (2,130ft)

PRINCIPAL HEIGHTS
Carn Dearg (Red Peak) 941m (3,089ft)

LOCH OSSIAN TO BRIDGE OF GAUR VIA CARN DEARG

LOCH OSSIAN YH TO CARN DEARG

(Allow 2¹/₂ hours)

Loch Ossian YH is a special resting place; this is not only because of its idyllic and remote location but also because of the relationship that Tom Rigg, the long-time warden, has forged with his visitors. Many photographs that have been taken in this area bear witness to the exceptionally tame red deer that inhabit the lochside, including, famously, one inquisitive deer which drops by to share meals with fellow hostelers. Wildlife lovers may thus suffer diminished food supplies, while those with athletic inclinations will be tempted by the unique challenge of the loch, on a circuit of international appeal (see Extensions, Stage 8).

Leave the YH on the track heading SSE, and at the junction with another follow the path opposite signposted 'Rannoch'. Soon after, turn left and pursue the path known to be part of 'The Road to the Isles'. As you ascend E, below Meall na Lice, it's worth the glance back to the mountains in the W.

From the boulder known as Peter's Rock, turn sharp left and walk N towards the top of a plantation. After about 150m (500ft), pick your own route over the heather up easy slopes of the hillside on your right. Stay E, avoiding the temptation of diversions along sheep tracks. Continue in that same direction from where the gradient eases, above about 650m (2,130ft). Further up, pass a tiny cairn perched on a boulder, followed by one or two similar stone piles, while slowly veering to the ESE.

Once on the rim of the Coire Creagach, follow a broad ridge SE to a high place strewn with rocks. The large cairn crowning the summit of Carn Dearg is an untypically neat pile of rock slabs. From it one can appreciate the great wilderness of Rannoch Moor. Both the Buachailles at Glen Coe, as well as the

117

STAGE 9

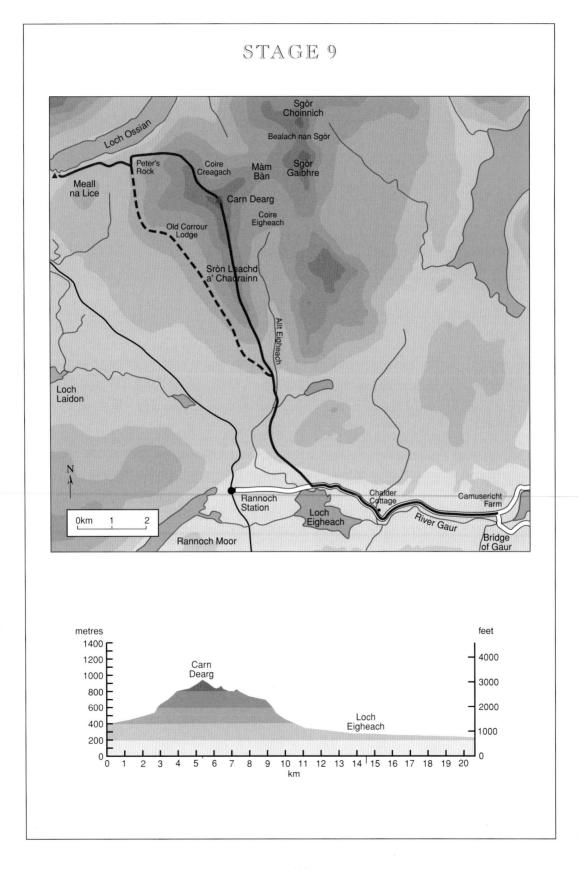

mountains of the White Corries, can be seen beyond Blackwater Reservoir. In the NE the distant bulk of Ben Alder overshadows the closer peaks (see Extensions). To the N lies still wilder country, with features including the impressive valley cut by the River Ossian, and there is much to appreciate in the Coire Creagach, a grassy bowl of rat-tail burns.

Carn Dearg to the Allt Eigheach

(Allow 2¼ hours)

Strike off SE from the summit to reach a smaller cairn after about 50m (160ft). Just beyond it, veer S and begin a traverse down the long, broad ridge above the Coire Eigheach. Along the way, the ridge dips to peaty depressions then rises again over bumps. Stay near or above 800m (2,625ft) for over 2km (1¼ miles). The traverse encounters a few rocky outcrops on terrain seemingly neglected by other walkers, where peace and solitude are almost guaranteed.

Approaching the southern end of the ridge, pass either side of a tiny lochan. On the other side of a grassy mound, walk down to pass to the left of a second lochan and out over Sròn Leachd a' Chaorainn. From here, descend more steeply, veering slightly to the E across peat spongy slopes. These are ideal conditions for the rare sundew; both the intermediate sundew and the great sundew flourish on this hill, but the sticky leaves of these tiny insectivorous plants would need to grow to triffid-like proportions to have any real effect on the midge population!

The gradient eases where the layers of vegetation underfoot thicken. Lower down, encounters with drainage cuttings and peat hags will cause only minor delays. At the bottom of the hill, join a track that leads E to a better track on the west bank of the Allt Eigheach. Follow the stream S for about 600m (1,950ft) to reach a timber foot-bridge at GR 435604.

Cross the bridge to the east bank of the Allt Eigheach and continue S by the farm track, heading towards hills that rise in gently rounded profiles so typical of the Grampians. Loch Laidon provides a silvery backdrop to the tiny hamlet at Rannoch Station. At the bottom of the track, by the road, a sign points back, confirming the route with which you are now familiar: 'Public Footpath to Fort William by Corrour'.

Carn Dearg, from the railway at Rannoch.

OVERLEAF

THE ALLT EIGHEACH TO CAMUSERICHT FARM

(Allow 2¾ hours)

Turn left and follow the B846 beside Loch Eigheach. The narrow lane, unfrequented by traffic, twists E down between grassy hillocks passing Chalder Cottage and the small hydroelectric power station. From here the day ends with a delightfully pleasant ramble beside the woods and water meadows in the valley of the River Gaur. Follow the road to just past the junction, signposted 'Bridge of Gaur ¼'. Camusericht Farm is on the right.

ALTERNATIVE ROUTES
LOW-LEVEL OPTION BELOW CARN DEARG
(Allow 6¼ hours)

From Loch Ossian YH begin as with the main route, by walking E up to Peter's Rock. Rather than continuing N and then E from here for the ascent of Carn Dearg, turn S and pursue the path that rises gently above the moor.

In summer, there is plenty of interesting flora to be found in the peaty banks and hollows. After about 1.5km (1 mile) beyond Peter's Rock, the path at 545m (1,798ft) comes near to its highest point. The route stays close to this altitude for some distance, affording prolonged views of Rannoch Moor. Further on, the distant volcano-like cone of Schiehallion appears, an unmistakable profile on the skyline to the ESE. Much closer at hand, the summit of Carn Dearg at the top of the broad corrie that rises on the left side is less eye-catching. It is noteworthy, however, that when other mountains are shrouded, Carn Dearg retains a remarkable reluctance to attract low cloud.

Passing to the right of what little remains of the ruined grey walls of Corrour Old Lodge, a wetter section is encountered. A few further intervening burns are forded easily by boulder-hopping. Below Sròn Leachd a' Chaorainn, the path veers E, flanking hill slopes used on the descent described from Carn Dearg. From just before the Allt Eigheach, the way to the Bridge of Gaur is shared with the main route.

ESCAPES

No curtailment is possible of the low-level route between Loch Ossian and the Bridge of Gaur. In emergencies, a telephone and assistance can be sought at Rannoch Station.

The high-level and low-level routes can each be conveniently undertaken as day trips, and private transport is not necessary. Disembark from the Fort William/Glasgow train at Corrour Station for Loch Ossian. On reaching the road by Loch Eigheach at the end of the day, simply turn right for Rannoch Station and the return train. The train service is not a frequent one, so consult timetables before setting out. For the high-level option, allow 6¼ hours; for the low-level option allow 5 hours.

EXTENSIONS

On this not unduly strenuous route, it is feasible for the fit to tackle the adjoining peaks, E of Carn Dearg, specifically Sgòr Gaibhre and Sgòr Choinnich. From Carn Dearg you should walk down NE, later veering ENE to the broad bealach of the Màm Bàn. Peat hags are encountered before the ascent begins on easier, mossy slopes leading to Sgòr Gaibhre and a finer view of remote Ben Alder. Those concerned solely with Munros can return to the Màm Bàn and descend the Coire Eigheach to gain the path beside the river of the same name.

To venture beyond and onto a third summit, first descend the steep ridge N from Sgòr Gaibhre to reach the Bealach nan Sgòr. From there, continue up to Sgòr Choinnich, returning the same way. Allow an extra 1½ hours for the Munro or 3 hours for both peaks.

Before commencing the main route, one of the very easiest ascents among Munros is possible on Beinn na Lap. From the YH, follow the track around the west end of Loch Ossian to reach the north side and from there climb N, on easy angled slopes, to gain a broad ridge. The summit is reached by walking ENE; return by the ascent route. Allow 3¼ hours to and from the YH.

The River Gaur near Bridge of Gaur.

OVERLEAF

STAGE 10
(LOW LEVEL)

BRIDGE OF GAUR TO GLEN LYON VIA
THE BLACK WOOD OF RANNOCH

MAP: OSLR 51

STARTING LOCATION
Camusericht Farm, GR 503571
Parking available by Loch Rannoch and in Glen Lyon

OVERVIEW/INTEREST
A route of varied landscapes, contrasting views and rare wildlife.
Explores a precious remnant of the ancient pine forest of Caledonia.
Finishes with an easy ramble in Scotland's longest and 'most beautiful' glen.
A long and quite demanding route.

FOOTPATHS
Good paths through the Black Wood and across the high moor.
Dry, level tracks and surfaced roads elsewhere.
Minimal waymarking.

GRADING: 3; high-level option, 4.

TIME ALLOWANCE: 8½ hours.

DISTANCE: 29.1km (18 miles)

TOTAL HEIGHT GAINED: 300m (985ft)

PRINCIPAL HEIGHTS
None, highest point at 490m (1,610ft) in the Lairig Ghallabaich.

Bridge of Gaur to Glen Lyon via the Black Wood of Rannoch

Bridge of Gaur to Rannoch School

(Allow 3¼ hours)

From Camusericht Farm, turn left and then left again, following the road over the Bridge of Gaur and past Georgetown Primary School. The broad hump that rises highest above the undulating moor to the S is Meall Buidhe, an unassuming Munro of little distinction. A rough track leads off towards it at the corner where the road veers left (see Extensions). However, continue NE, passing the tiny Braes of Rannoch Parish Church at the edge of a field where Highland cattle may be seen. If you look across the flat meadows on your left, Loch Rannoch comes into view.

Follow the lane above Finnart Farm to come down by the loch at the bottom of a large birch wood. Opposite Finnart Lodge, the pipelines of Killichonan Hydro Power Station are a somewhat incongruous sight on a hill slope above the north shore. Protruding from the waters of the loch is the tiny Crannog (artificial island dwelling) of Eilean nam Faoileag; MacDougal of Lorne, Chief of the clan MacDougal, was once imprisoned in its tower. Other tales recalling local clan history can be found on a Clan Trail information board by the loch shore. This spot, taking in the view across the water, is just right for a brief pause.

Between an extensive spread of silver birch trees on the right side of the road and the south shore of the loch on the left, a pleasant, normally traffic-free ramble is guaranteed as you progress E. After Croiscrag House, walk on over the bridge that crosses the Allt Camghouran and out across an area of open fields. When about 1.2km (¾ mile) E of the bridge, opposite a small lay-by and just beyond Blackwood Lodge, leave the road, taking a path up into the trees on the right, heading S.

This forest has a very different character from anything so far encountered on

STAGE 10

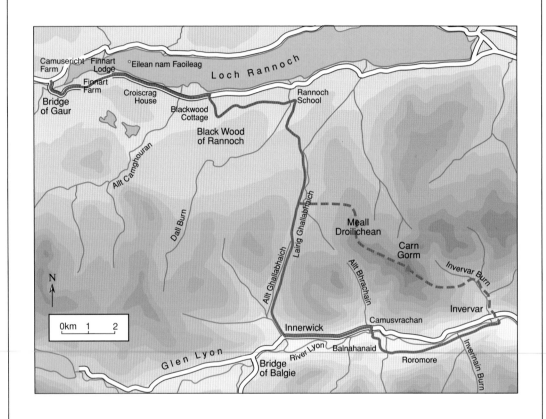

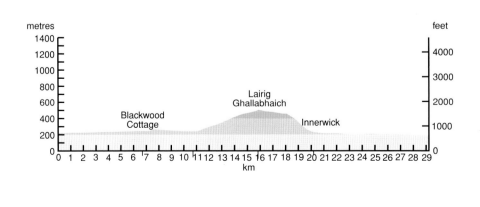

the Highland Round. The trees are predominantly Scots pine, and, protected from grazing, the ground layer is a mix of mature heather, juniper and pine saplings that have been allowed to establish since being designated an SSSI in 1955. It is a rare and special place, a precious fragment that offers a hint of what the ancient forest of Caledonia must have once looked like, before our demand for timber reduced its extent to less than 1 per cent of the country. It is on record that if the First World War had not ended in 1918, all of the Black Wood of Rannoch would have been felled. There is hope that in this wood one may glimpse the future as well as the past. Thankfully, since 1975 it has been protected and enhanced by a plan that aims to preserve the Rannoch strain of Scots pine. The result of these efforts is the opportunity to observe native wildlife in a forest that puts to shame the regimented plantations nearby.

The path soon joins a wider one rising from behind the lodge cottages. Turn left and continue uphill into the trees, staying alert to the rare creatures that can be seen, such as the red squirrel, the Scottish crossbill and the capercaillie.

After 1km (⅔ mile) and, before a clearing on the right, veer ENE, passing to the right of a densely wooded enclosure. Further on, having lost a few metres' altitude, turn right at the junction of paths and go uphill again. Where the path divides, after about 300m (1000ft), take the left fork and continue through the Black Wood, heading E. In this section, invasive birch scrub has succeeded in becoming more established. The path terminates at a more obvious forestry track. Turn left and walk downhill, leaving the Blackwood just before crossing the bridge on the right over the Dall Burn. You will soon emerge by a row of new cottages, near the grounds of Rannoch School.

RANNOCH SCHOOL TO INNERWICK

(Allow 2¾ hours)

Without entering the school grounds, walk uphill by the track on the right, beginning opposite the third cottage along. This follows the east bank of the Dall Burn, at the edge of the plantation, heading SSW. At a more frequented forestry access track, after about 1.2km (¾ mile), turn left. Where the track divides almost immediately, take the right fork and follow it around to reach the east side of a lochan. Continue S from here to reach a crossroads of paths and tracks and follow the sign to 'Glen Lyon'. After a further 2km (1¼ miles), when at the southern edge of the Rannoch Forest plantations, pass through a k-gate and out onto the open moor.

Walk SSW from the forest edge, across the wet moorland on a rough path, which is marked as a track on OS maps. Higher up in the Lairig Ghallabhaich, the heather-thick

hillslopes on both sides of the Allt Ghallabhaich confine your passage. Follow the track, staying above the east side of the burn. After entering the plantation area, ignore a rising track off to the left. Instead, continue down, more steeply at a hairpin bend, to emerge from the trees next to the stream. Veer left, away from the bankside and stay close to the edge of the forest.

The track soon comes next to the east bank of a wider river, now enlarged by the combined forces of two streams. Join the road in Glen Lyon opposite a small church, at a point immediately E of a War Memorial.

In the Black Wood of Rannoch.

INNERWICK TO INVERVAR
(Allow 2¹/₂ hours)

Turn left and follow the Glen Lyon road to Camusvracan, which is a pleasant rural ramble on a country lane beside the river. Glen Lyon is best seen from the south side of the river, so from Camusvracan take the track leading off to the right, beginning between a cottage and the bridge over the Allt Bhrachain. Cross the bridge at the River Lyon, walk on over a cattle-grid and turn left, passing the farm at Balnahanaid and soon after the new house at Roromore. Beyond the farm at Roromore the track is more overgrown as you enter a copse of hazel scrub.

It would be foolish to hurry through this, Scotland's longest glen. Linger among tranquil meadows and woods and beside picturesque banks and quaint bridges. Postcards confidently echo the assertions of locals that Glen Lyon is Scotland's most beautiful glen. Perhaps a few would argue otherwise, but it is a tame rural beauty very different from the high drama and solemnity that so captures the imagination in Glen Coe (Stage 6).

The pretty scenes continue when below the plantation area, walking ENE on the right side of a broken wall. Some way beyond the hump-back bridge that crosses the Inverinain Burn the track terminates in attractive woods above the river. A better track then leads down to the left, over a sturdy bridge at the river and on to the Glen Lyon road. The driveway leading to Invervar Lodge is opposite.

ALTERNATIVE ROUTES
HIGH-LEVEL OPTION VIA CARN GORM
(Allow 9 hours)

Follow the main route as far as the open moor at GR 594525. Having emerged at the top of Rannoch Forest, leave the path and strike off E across the grass and heather. Climb a steepening slope leading to the ridge at Meall Droilichean, at the same time veering away from the forest perimeter fencing on the left.

Turn S to reach two cairns, specially sculptured for wind protection, on the ridge at about 830m (2,725ft). From the easternmost cairn, walk ESE to a high and sparse plateau-like area from where the continued ascent of a broad lichen- and moss-covered ridge leads up to the fallen triangular pillar of Carn Gorm. An encircling windbreak affords some

The River Lyon at Roromore, Glen Lyon.

OVERLEAF

respite from relentless westerly winds, while the highest point of the summit is marked by the cairn located a few metres to the SE. Of particular note is the fine view back across Loch Rannoch.

Up to three further Munro summits can be ticked off by pursuing the long, broad grassy ridge that arcs around to the east of Carn Gorm. Straightforward descents, on the southern side, can be made from almost any point along it, but given that you will have walked 22.5km (14 miles) since breakfast, this will not be in many minds.

Leave Carn Gorm by its east ridge, at first descending SE. The upper reaches of the corrie on your left reveal an untypically rugged scene for hills where such descriptions do not come easily to mind. Views ahead begin to reveal something of the beauty of lower Glen Lyon.

On reaching the Invervar Burn, stay close to the forest edge, next to a fence line heading down to a foot-bridge. Cross to the east bank and follow the burn down to meet the road, opposite an old red telephone box. Turn right for the driveway that leads up to Invervar Lodge.

ESCAPES

Other than pursuing the lochside road all the way to Rannoch School or continuing on the tarmac surface in Glen Lyon after Camusvracan, there are no practical curtailments of this route. In any case, both the above options shave only minutes off the time allocation and in no way justify missing some of the finest aspects of the route in the Black Wood of Rannoch and in Glen Lyon.

CURTAILMENT OF HIGHLAND ROUND

By omitting the traverse of the Lawers Range (Stage 11), it is possible to combine Stages 10 and 11 into one very long day. Take the road through the pass between Glen Lyon and Loch Tay, to reach the track beginning 1.2km (¾ mile) S of the Lawers Dam, as described at the end of Stage 11. Allow 5¼ hours between Innerwick and Killin.

EXTENSIONS

The suggested extension is recommended for anyone who is prepared to add 5km (3 miles) to this already long route. From the Bridge of Gaur, it avoids the tarmac beside Loch Rannoch at the start of the day.

Turn left off the road a few metres after Georgetown Primary School and follow the rising track S over the open moor, walking towards the hump-like profile of Meall

Buidhe. At a cairn on the left after 3km (2 miles), leave the track for a grassy path around the south side of Leagag. The rocky north face of Cross Craigs is directly ahead and, being the most rugged feature around, is easily identified. The scene across the valley of the Luban Féith a' Mhadaidh is one of wild remoteness.

As you descend, pick up the track beside the west bank of the Allt Camghouran and follow it downstream, skirting the edge of an attractive mixed forest. Before joining the road by Loch Rannoch, 1.3km (¾ mile) W of Blackwood Lodge (Cottage on map), some very fine stands of Scots pine are encountered above the river bank. You should allow an extra 1½ hours.

A less strenuous diversion is via the riverside beauty spot at the Bridge of Balgie, in Glen Lyon. This picturesque hamlet lies 1.6km (1 mile) W along the road from Inner-wick, where there is an art gallery displaying paintings of local scenes. Close by, the Post Office proprietor, Kate Conway, serves tea and snacks. Cross the bridge and pick up the 'Kerrowmore' track which later joins the main route on the south side of the river by Camusvracan. You should allow an extra hour of this extension.

STAGE 11
(HIGH LEVEL)

GLYN LYON TO KILLIN VIA BEN LAWERS

MAP: OSLR 51

STARTING LOCATION
Invervar Lodge, Glen Lyon, GR 667484
Parking possible in Glen Lyon and at NTS Visitor Centre

OVERVIEW/INTEREST
Traverse of a magnificent high-level ridge, involving over 1542m (5,000ft) of ascent.
Far-reaching views from the summits of five Munros, including the highest mountain
in the Southern Highlands, renowned for its rare flora.
From 1 August to 30 January contact the estate keeper (01887) 877233 in Glen Lyon.
Extremely demanding route on the most challenging day of the round.

FOOTPATHS
Barely distinguishable path on an unfrequented ascent but mostly follows a fence line.
Path on main ridge is over varied terrain, steep in places.
Scrambling necessary on An Stùic; seriously eroded 'tourist path' on descent.
Good Land Rover track followed by long 'stairway' descent to Killin.
No waymarking.

GRADING: 6; low-level option, 3.

TIME ALLOWANCE: 10¼ hours

DISTANCE: 23.2km (14½ miles)

TOTAL HEIGHT GAINED: 1,650m (5,410ft)

PRINCIPAL HEIGHTS
Ben Lawers (Loud Mountain) 1,214m (3,982ft)
Meall Garbh (Rough Hill) 1,118m (3,667ft)
An Stùic (The Peak) 1,118m (3,667ft)
Meall Greigh (Hill of Horse Studs) 1,001m (3,285ft)
Beinn Ghlas (Green Hill) 1,103m (3,620ft)

Glen Lyon to Killin via Ben Lawers

Invervar to Meall Greigh
(Allow 3 hours)

Beginning opposite the lodge driveway, take the track heading S from Invervar. Walk back over the bridge at the River Lyon, retracing the route at the end of Stage 10, but then continue to the farm at Dericambus. Go through a gate on the left for access to a path that zigzags S up the hillside. Ignore any unwelcoming or intimidating notices displayed by the South Chesthill Estate, especially those attempting to discourage access to the hills (except during the stalking season; see Overview/Interest).

On reaching the top of a tree-lined ravine near Creag Dhubh, follow a path SW through the heather to find a fence at the top of a grassy depression. Then turn left and follow the line of fencing up slopes leading to a broad ridge that swings S towards the now-visible summit of Meall Greigh. It is a simple matter to follow the fence in that direction.

Near the top, a fairly steep climb leads up to the fence line on the main ridge, a few hundred metres (yards) west of the summit. Walk out SE, passing the small cairn lower down before arriving at the true summit, the most easterly point not only of Stage 11 but of the entire Highland Round. As one might expect, the view E, beyond Loch Tay, is across much lower, more fertile country. However, the real virtue of this summit is its position in relation to the corrie surrounding Lochan nan Cat. The view of the ridges and peaks leading on to Ben Lawers, especially after the tiring climb out of Glen Lyon, is inspirational.

Meall Greigh to Ben Lawers
(Allow 3¼ hours)

Leave the summit and, at first, head WNW. Continue the descent of an easy-angled

STAGE 11

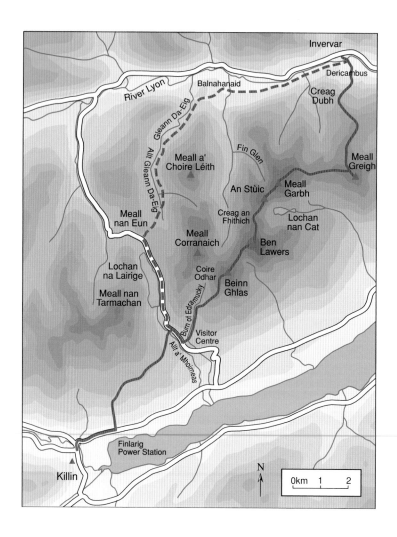

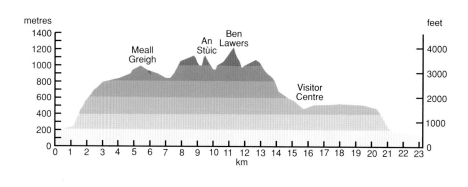

slope, veering W and keeping to the left side of the fence along the high ridge. This quiet part of the Lawers range is a favourite haunt for ptarmigan. Rarely venturing below about 760m (2,500ft), these residents of the sparsely vegetated tops are not easily observed. Seasonal variations in coloration, appropriate to the degree of snow cover, ensure that the birds are camouflaged in an environment where the eagle sees all and hiding places are difficult to find. Snow buntings also frequent these tops.

Walk uphill from the col at 830m (2,725ft), keeping next to a fence line that is breached by a few rudimentary stiles, allowing a path that alternates from one side to the other to be followed. For the most part, the steep ascent of Meall Garbh is WNW, but where the gradient eases, bear SW. As you approach from the E, there appear to be two separate summits. However, it is the small cairn perched on the more northerly top that marks the higher, true summit at 1,118m (3,668ft). Meall Garbh is another fine viewpoint. From here, the prospect of continuing along the ridge towards Ben Lawers may seem daunting, but the way up over the sharp cone of An Stùic might be a more immediate cause for apprehension.

Having bagged your second Munro of the day, leave the summit, heading SSW along a short, narrow ridge before commencing a steep descent on a well-worn path leading to the col before An Stùic. Take care between rocky outcrops on the way down.

Once at the base of An Stùic, a path off to the right bypasses the peak and avoids the very steep climb on its rugged northeast face (see Escapes). Those committed to the challenge should begin the ascent by the path that twists up over the rocks with abrupt steepness. Some easy scrambling is necessary before the summit cairn is reached on this peak recently promoted to a Munro. While An Stùic is a challenging obstacle, the capable will find it an exhilarating, not least for the prize of the summit itself, precipitously perched as it is above Lochan nan Cat. The shape of lochan looks like a sitting cat. The crowning glory of the traverse, Ben Lawers, now seems quite close.

Commence a descent down the less severe, grassy south side of the peak. The col at the bottom is reached without difficulty, and the An Stùic bypass path there rejoins the path along the crest of the ridge. The climbing begins again. Clamber over rocks at Creag an Fhithich to reach a boulder plateau. From here, the ascent continues S for a final, gruelling pull up to the summit of Ben Lawers.

Glen Lyon, on the ascent S from Invervar.

OVERLEAF

At 1,214m (3,983ft), Ben Lawers is the highest mountain in the Southern Highlands. From the top, weather permitting, it is possible to look down on most of the other summits encountered on the Highland Round, giving an encouraging sense of the distance that has been covered. The magnificent panorama entirely befits its lofty status, extending across 130° of the compass. From SW to N, Ben More, Stob Binnein, Ben Lui and Ben Nevis are among the many peaks vying for attention. On a good day, and on a distant horizon, the Cairngorm plateau is clearly identifiable.

Just a few metres N of the triangulation point lie the diminished ruins of what was once a huge summit tower. Today, its scattered remains serve merely as a memorial to the failed efforts of enthusiasts to add 20 feet to the mountain, thus distinguishing it as one of the elite 'Scottish Fours'.

BEN LAWERS TO KILLIN
(Allow 4 hours)

Ben Lawers has a special place in my memory as the site of an extraordinary phenomenon of the mountains, known as the 'broken spectra'. The phenomenon entails seeing one's shadow projected onto a mist by a low sun, quite surreal in itself, although exaggerated by viewing that shadow surrounded by successive 'glories' (halos) of rainbows. The effect is a fantastically strange vision, disturbing enough in some instances to have led mountaineers to tell of 'supernatural' or 'holy' encounters. The sense of being divinely chosen or special is enhanced by the revelation that, while you might also see your companions' shadows in the mist you can only ever see the colourful spectra around your own!

A well-worn, unmistakable footpath allows for a rapid drop of more than 200m (656ft) to be made on the west side before the last summit of the day. A gradual climb SSW, involving a final ascent of 100m (330ft) leads to the cairnless summit of the fifth Munro of the day. From Beinn Ghlas, Ben Lawers assumes a broad pyramidal form while, towards Glen Lyon, a corrie drops precipitously away.

Continue SW, beyond summit outcrops, to reach a cairn after about 100m (330ft). The descent is quite steep from here over rocks, which, after the soaking of a spring thaw, are typically wet and easily dislodged. A succession of further cairns proves unnecessary in marking a path down to a less steep, broader section of the ridge. Bear S to pass a large cairn, then SW again, keeping to the well-defined path over the grass. This path has become a seriously eroded scar on the mountainside, testimony to the popularity of Ben Lawers and the ease and convenience of the ascent from the NTS Visitor Centre.

The path joins with one on the right, from Coire Odhar, just before you reach the ladder-stile over deer fencing on the edge of the nature reserve. From here, follow the Burn of Edramucky downstream. Help to prevent unnecessary disturbance of rare plants by respecting the NTS signs directing you to the car park. In summer, the reserve is a very special place for botanists, and among the unusual flora that thrive in these alkaline-rich soils are alpine forget-me-nots, purple saxifrage, alpine gentian and snow pearlwort.

Leave the southern end of the fenced area by another high stile, walking out over the boardwalk to the Visitor Centre. It is difficult to view the Visitor Centre building and car park as anything other that blots on the landscape. Few would doubt the value of information and interpretation centres, but the example on Ben Lawers is proof that half-way up a mountain is not the right place.

Walk NE along the road from the car park, leaving it for a Land Rover track off to the left after about 0.5km (⅓ mile). Cross the Allt a' Mhoirneas by the concrete bridge and continue SW on the gently rising track. In winter and spring snow tends to accumulate and linger on the hard-pack surface, but the route is easily followed. The track skirts below the heather-clad slopes of Meall nan Tarmachan until it divides after about 3km (2 miles). Take the left fork, heading gently downhill to its terminus at a grey building on the top of a hydroelectric pipeline. Turn S and follow a disused narrow-gauge railway downhill, on the left side of the pipeline. Old concrete sleepers serve as a good staircase on the steeper sections. Pass through two separate copses of mixed trees on the way down – any intervening fencing is easily crossed – before reaching a buffer at the bottom. From here, a tarmac track leads to a metal gate at the A827 after 250m (800ft). Turn right and walk for 2km (1¼ miles) by the roadside, passing Finlarig Power Station, a golf course and Glen Lochay Hotel before reaching Killin YH. For those seeking a quiet night, free of snoring hostelers, numerous B&Bs are situated in the village further down the road.

ALTERNATIVE ROUTES
LOW-LEVEL OPTION VIA GLEANN DA-EIG
(Allow 7¼ hours)

From the bridge over the River Lyon, located just S of Invervar Lodge, gain the track heading WSW back through the glen, in reverse of the end of the main route suggested for Stage 10. Leave that track by a rough track that goes SW from Balnahanaid, ascending slopes scattered with numerous outcrops. Though wet in places, the track is easy to follow well up into the Gleann Dà-Eig. As you gain height, fine views are to be had looking back E into Glen Lyon. Once above the Allt Gleann Dà-Eig, ignore a track off to the right and, instead, continue upstream.

The moorland on the west side is heather-covered, while on the near slopes grass cover gives a contrasting impression of colour and tone. Higher up, closer to the burn, the glen is increasingly confined by enclosing hill slopes, until the track veers S before finally fading to insignificance. From here, it is necessary to freerange S across the damp and open moor.

The burn is easily forded but then you must begin a tiresome slog across heather, aiming for the dip on the skyline between Meall nan Eun and a slightly higher mound on the left. Once there, having maintained a bearing of 190°, go down through a long grassy depression to emerge at the roadside about 80m (250ft) to the E of a large cairn at GR 594417. This stone pile marks the summit of the road through the pass.

Turn left and follow the road S, beside Lochan na Lairige. Continue by the track leading out to the hydroelectric pipeline above Killin. It begins 1.2km (¾ mile) S of the Lawers Dam and is described in the main route.

ESCAPES

When the mountains are misted out, the fence line between Meall Greigh and Meall Garbh prevents navigational errors on this part of the ridge. However, unless you are well practised in the accurate use of map and compass, do not proceed beyond Meall Garbh in such conditions. The safer option is to follow the fence line back E, to just before the col, and from here descend SE to the small dam at the top of the Lawers Burn. A path leads downstream to Lawers and the A827.

It is also possible to descend the southern slopes of Meall Greigh, picking up the Lawers Burn further down. As an alternative route to the 'tourist path' from Ben Lawers' summit, it is possible to descend its east ridge to reach the village of Lawers via the same burn.

On the north side of the range it is possible to return to Glen Lyon by one of two ridges descending Meall Garbh. These can also be used as ascent routes, omitting Meall Greigh. I have yet to explore it myself, but Fin Glen may well provide a practicable link between Camusvracan in Glen Lyon and An Stùic. Unfortunately, as descent routes, none of the alternatives mentioned above is convenient for finishing the day at Killin. A small saving of energy and time (30 minutes) can be achieved by omitting the summit of Meall Greigh. Make a detour SW from the fence line at GR 669448, having followed it

Trig pillar on the summit of Ben Lawers.

up as described in the main route, to join the ridge just E of the col below Meall Greigh.

From the Visitor Centre, the road alternative down to Killin avoids the steep descent by the hydroelectric pipeline but has neither a distance nor a time advantage.

The quickest route to the summit of Ben Lawers is by the well-trodden 'tourist path' from the Visitor Centre, via Beinn Ghlas. Beginning with a 430m (1,410ft) head-start up the mountain, the return route is a short day. Allow 5 hours.

EXTENSIONS

Stage 11 is, by any standards, a long and challenging day. The pursuit of additional mileage or climbing would place unreasonable demands on energy levels of even the

toughest hillwalkers and is, therefore, not practicable. However, in theory, the hardened might push on to complete the 12km (8-mile) Lawers ridge by continuing from Beinn Ghlas over the two remaining Munros, Meall Corranaich and Meall a' Choire Léith.

Beinn Ghlas, Meall Corranaich and beyond from Ben Lawers.

STAGE 12
(LOW LEVEL)

KILLIN TO GLEN DOCHART VIA THE FALLS OF DOCHART

MAP: OSLR 51

STARTING LOCATION
Killin YH, GR 571339

Parking available in Killin

OVERVIEW/INTEREST
A pleasant ramble along the course of a dismantled railway.

Visits the popular beauty spot at the spectacular Falls of Dochart.

A varied walk through a forest as well as out along the open glen.

Straightforward and undemanding route.

FOOTPATHS
Firm, dry and level on the trackbed of an old railway.

Wetter underfoot west of the forest.

Involves a river crossing, which is straightforward in normal conditions.

No waymarking.

GRADING: 2. If river crossing avoided, 1; high-level option, 4.

TIME ALLOWANCE: 3¾ hours

DISTANCE: 11.8km (7¼ miles)

TOTAL HEIGHT GAINED: 150m (490ft)

PRINCIPAL HEIGHTS
None; highest point is 230m (755ft) at GR 527283.

KILLIN TO GLEN DOCHART VIA THE FALLS OF DOCHART

KILLIN YH TO LIX TOLL

(Allow 1¼ hours)

Rejuvenated after the Lawers marathon by a good night's sleep, walk through the village and leave Killin via the bridge over the River Dochart. The falls are a popular beauty spot, one of Scotland's most photographed sites, and spectacular when in spate. Walk beside the A87, following the River Dochart upstream for 300m (1000ft). Turn left, just before a memorial, and take a track leading to a small swing gate set inside a much larger one. Walk under a bridge on the right, following the course of a dismantled railway, the Killin branch of the old Callander and Oban line.

Embankments on each side of the trackbed are pleasantly wooded with birch, ash and rowan. Make your way SW on this level and dry route, the absence of gradient aiding rapid progress. Piles of old, moss-covered sleepers are clues to the existence of the railway that closed in 1965. Views to your right across Glen Dochart and to the hills on the north side can be enjoyed in gaps between the trees. Pass a moss-covered stone wall on your right, where Meall Clachach is seen across the slate roof tiles of Acharn Farm cottages (see High-level Option).

Continue along the dismantled railway track between the conifers. Splashes of colour in autumn are provided by a scattering of birch, a welcome deciduous invasion of the forest edge that was kept clear in pre-Beeching days to allow the passage of steam. Further on, pass over a stream flowing through a small wood of oak, ash and birch. In autumn, all along the embankment, redwings and fieldfares can often be seen gorging themselves on the rowan berries.

Pass beneath the pylons, enjoying, before they are obscured by maturing spruce, views SW into Glen Dochart. The impressive outlines of the Tarmachan Ridge and the Ben Lawers range above Killin are visible on your right.

149

STAGE 12

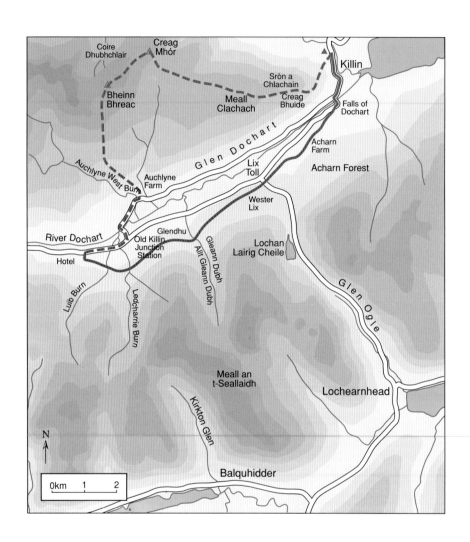

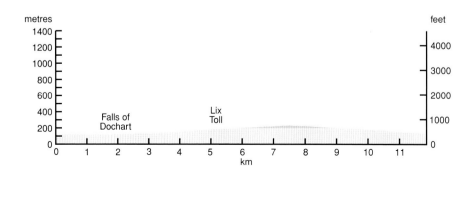

At MR 555308 continue straight on at a junction of tracks, entering a section somewhat overgrown and neglected and where the route is reduced to a path. Go through a wooden k-gate between deer fencing and pass over a bridge crossing a fast-flowing woodland burn. The route becomes less confined and resumes along the open railway trackbed. Just before the A85 at Lix Toll, go round a low metal barrier, which prevents vehicular access.

LIX TOLL TO LUIB HOTEL
(Allow 2½ hours)

Cross the road bearing right to regain the course of the dismantled railway, and continue SW on entering a mature plantation. This section through Acharn Forest is rather typical of plantation tracks, complete with views obscured by monotonous conifers, although there is more deciduous diversity further on. From Lix Toll, progress continues on a good surface. The long fronds of some forest ferns enliven the banks of a burn near a clearing in front of the white building at Wester Lix, while a brief glimpse to Ben More and Stob Binnein provides further interest. Also visible, across the tops of the conifers, is the indistinct summit of Sgiath Chùil, a Munro on the north side of Glen Dochart. Note that timber-felling operations may result in some diversions.

Looking up to your left, you will see an old bridge that once carried the railway from Glen Ogle, the course of which joins from that side. Further examples of the railway architecture of the past can be seen in the sad, eerie ruins of neglected railway cottages at the old Killin Junction Station. Towards the far west end of the plantation area rhododendron – like bracken, an ever-encroaching threat to Scotland's natural flora – is gaining an unwelcome foothold at the trackside.

Just after a horse chestnut tree on the right, cross the Allt Gleann Dubh by a long, high bridge at the edge of the forest. If you look up the glen to the S, you will just discern the triangulation pillar on Meall an t-Seallaidh. The view N to W is now quite extensive across Glen Dochart, to the Breadalbane hills beyond.

On the other side of the bridge, pass through a wooden gate. Ignoring a track off to left, bear right and head W passing under a railway arch. A tiny railway shed constructed of old sleepers might provide a useful lunch stop in bad weather. A scattering of willow on each side warns of wetter ground underfoot as you continue along the raised course of the railway. On resuming a SW bearing, pass through a wooden gate after skirting a large hole in the trackbed. At a small plantation on your left, the broad glen and the meandering River Dochart are clearly visible on the right. Step over a low wooden barrier at a small concrete bridge over a burn and then go under the single cable of an electric fence, suspended 3m (10ft) off the ground. You will come across a second concrete bridge soon after. Ben More and Stob Binnein now feature more prominently ahead of you.

Bear WSW, passing over a long bridge under which flows the Ledcharrie Burn. Continue between tree-lined embankments, curving around WNW on a gravelly surface to reach the Luib Burn at wooden fencing. The old bridge over the burn has collapsed, and so it is now necessary to ford the burn, best achieved by walking downstream a little way and crossing there. In normal conditions this should involve no more than removing your socks and boots. If it is in spate, see Escapes.

Having crossed the burn, walk up the embankment to regain the track and continue WNW, coming closer to the pylons again on your right. Bear W to reach the tiny bridge situated immediately S of the Luib Hotel, a low white building easily seen across the field to your right. Walk down the left side of the raised bank, passing under the railway. Then walk N, directly towards the Luib Hotel, across the grassy moor to reach an electrified perimeter fence. Pass under the fence at the section protected by rubber and then through a old lichen-encrusted gate to reach the roadside. The Luib Hotel is opposite.

ALTERNATIVE ROUTES
HIGH-LEVEL OPTION VIA BHEINN BHREAC
(Allow 6½ hours)

Start from the back of Killin YH and walk WSW up towards the trees. Pick up a rough track, which leads through to the pylons beyond. On reaching a dry-stone wall, turn left and then follow the power lines to a wooden gate at the top, bracken-infested corner of the field.

Continue S, below the more westerly of the power lines, towards a grassy hillock. From here, a ridge path ascends W over the outcrops at Sròn a Chlachain and onto the summit of Creag Bhuide (not marked on OSLR series maps). Here there are three prominent cairns, the most easterly offering a fantastic vantage point for views across Loch Tay. The true summit is at a cairn lying about 130m (425ft) further W from where one can enjoy fine views across Glen Dochart as well as back to the Lawers range and the Tarmachans. From here, walk W for approximately 2km (1¼ miles) across the open heather moor towards the higher top of Meall Clachach. Its probably best to attempt a banana-shaped

The Falls of Dochart, Killin.

sweep around to the left to reach the summit. Continue WNW, ranging freely across rough, stumble-inducing heathery clumps, peat hags and wet pools, attempting to aim below and just to the left of Creag Mhór. When you are immediately below the summit, cross a burn and climb up the steep southeast-facing slope to reach the top. Although there is no cairn on the grassy summit itself, there is a small folly of concrete blocks a few metres down on the north side. Pause to enjoy the panorama of Breadalbane mountains stretching along the north side of Glen Lochy.

For even better views, head SW along the fragmented and non-distinct ridge leading to Bheinn Bhreac. Approaching this highest summit of the day, you will reach a folly of a similar style to the one encountered at Creag Mhór. Possibly the finest aspect of Bheinn Bhreac, though, exists in the immediate surroundings, especially in the ambience that prevails at the Coire Dhubhchlair. The presence of a tiny lochan at the top of the corrie, below and to the immediate W, should alleviate any doubts about navigational errors.

Push on S, from Bheinn Bhreac, taking care at first as you descend the crags below the summit. The downhill gradient steepens before you pick up the track flanking the hillside. Find the junction with the one that heads SE down to Auchlyne Farm.

At the bottom, turn right and cross the bridge over Auchlyne West Burn and follow the minor road over the River Dochart to join the A85 at Ledcharrie. The Luib Hotel is nearly 1.5km (1 mile) further W.

ESCAPES

The route along the course of the railway is level and easy to follow, and the only real obstacle is the crossing of the Luib Burn. During spells of high water, this problem can be overcome by walking out N to the main road at Ledcharrie.

The quiet minor road from Killin, on the north side of Glen Dochart, offers the quickest walking route to Luib – a tarmac lane, but one that is unfrequented by traffic. There are plenty of picturesque views, too: a lovely river and a fine mountain backdrop dominated by Ben More and Stob Binnein. The road joins the A85 at Ledcharrie, just E of the Luib Hotel. Allow 3 hours.

EXTENSIONS

For those not feeling too tired after the Lawers traverse (Stage 11), the high-level option has much to recommend it. However, because of the awkward terrain on the high moor, and because of the potential navigational problems of traversing a poorly defined ridge, it is a route best avoided in mist.

Desires to extend the main route itself are perhaps best indulged by exploring one of the three glens leading S from Glen Dochart. The most easterly of these, Glenogle, can be reached along any of a number of forest tracks to the S of Killin. From Glenogle Cottages, the trackbed of the old Callander line can be followed along the west side of the glen to Lochearnhead. A return is possible by a nature trail on the other side. From Lochan Lairig Cheile, continue N and W along the course of the old railway, later joining the main route again at Glendhu. Allow an extra 5 hours.

Quieter diversions, well away from traffic, are possible in Gleann Dubh, and these can be explored at will by the path on the east side of the burn. A more popular diversion, however, is along the path to Balquhidder from Ledcharrie, waymarked via the Kirkton Glen. Return by the same path. Allow an extra 5½ hours.

Dawn at Glen Dochart.

OVERLEAF

STAGE 13
HIGH LEVEL

GLEN DOCHART TO CRIANLARICH VIA BEN MORE

MAP: OSLR 50 and 51

STARTING LOCATION
Luib Hotel, Glen Dochart, GR 494279
Parking at the lay-by, GR 455277

OVERVIEW/INTEREST
A fitting finish to the Round on the highest mountain in Britain south of Strath Tay.
Magnificent vistas over much of the Southern and Central Highlands, from the summits
of two Munros.
An unfrequented ascent to an otherwise popular summit.
Demanding physically due to height gained.

FOOTPATHS
Good forest track on approach.
Some free-ranging necessary on unpathed mountain sides.
Steep and well-worn path on ridge traverse between the two peaks.
No waymarking.

GRADING: 4; low-level option, 3.

TIME ALLOWANCE: 8¼ hours

DISTANCE: 19.1km (11¾ miles)

TOTAL HEIGHT GAINED: 1,400m (4,590ft)

PRINCIPAL HEIGHTS
Ben More (Big Mountain) 1,174m (3,851ft)
Stob Binnein (Anvil Peak) 1,164m (3,822ft)

Glen Dochart to Crianlarich via Ben More

Luib to Ben More
(Allow 4¼ hours)

To those who know the area, Ben More and Stob Binnein are familiar landmarks that, together, present a fine twinning of peaks. Viewed from almost any direction, they have a commanding presence, befitting their great height and bulk. The traverse of both is one of the more popular objectives of a day spent in the Southern Highlands, although many walkers opt for the return trip from Benmore Farm, via an ascent on the northwestern slopes (see Escapes). This route has the advantage of directness, but it lacks the interest of an approach from the eastern side.

A combination of neglect, prohibitive fencing, road improvements and an unsympathetic caravan-site owner have conspired to render impracticable any notions of continuing from Luib along the trackbed of the dismantled railway. There are plans for a Central Highland Way (for cyclists and pedestrians), permitting unhindered passage through Glen Dochart, but at present it is necessary to walk at the roadside when venturing west of the Luib Hotel. The one saving grace of this route is that of speed in reaching the foot of Ben More. Keeping a brisk pace, one need suffer no more than an hour on the highway.

After 4km (2½ miles) leave the roadside at a gate on the left (GR 457276), just E of the Allt Coire Chaorach. Follow a rough track S to a stile at the plantation edge, and from here head up to where the track divides in the coniferous gloom of the plantation. Take the right fork of the track and cross the Allt Coire Chaorach by means of the stepping stones. Bear left on the opposite bank, following a solid track on a rising gradient to emerge from the spruce a little way beyond a burn in a forest clearing. Follow the plantation edge around to the left at first, but soon veer out towards the open hillside, heading SW and then W towards Ben More's northeastern ridge. As you come closer to a fence line, follow its course upward to ford a burn. From the other side,

159

STAGE 13

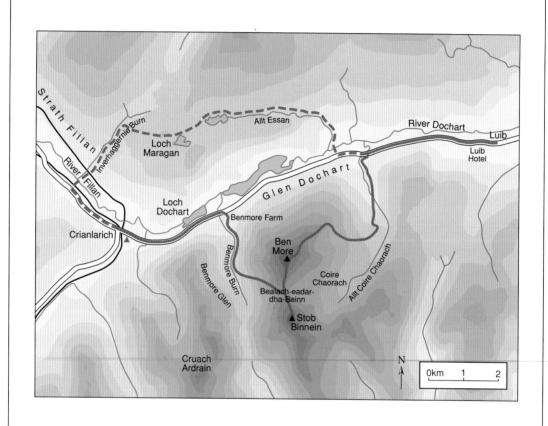

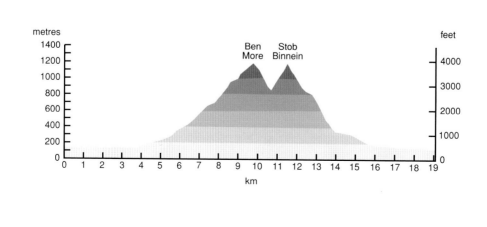

proceed along a line of defunct fence posts, which lead NW onto the crest of the ridge.

There are, in places, the faint traces of a path on the ridge, which rises SW. However, while the ascent continues from here on more rugged terrain it presents few problems. The more extensive of any lingering snow pockets can be avoided on the left side, and thoughtful deliberation about the best route will avoid any loss of height. The panorama of peaks to the W and N, as well as the sight of the vast water-sodden depression of the Coire Chaorach below, are reasons for lingering on the way up.

As you approach the summit, the profiles of other walkers on the right side of the hill will identify a slope endured by Munroists on a less imaginative route. The narrowing ridge becomes less steep, as a path over moss and between schistose slabs leads, at last, to the summit cairn on Ben More. From here, the fantastic view is seemingly across half of Scotland in what will, for those finishing the Round, be an all-encompassing display that prompts happy recollections of a memorable fortnight. Less familiar perhaps, but closer and abutting Benmore Glen, Cruach Ardrain is clearly visible to the SSW. More prominent among neighbouring peaks is Stob Binnein, which has yet to be climbed. The Stob is the slightly junior, yet more elegant partner of this favourite duo and, as the eagle flies, just a tempting 2km (1¼ miles) from Ben More.

BEN MORE TO STOB BINNEIN
(Allow 1 hour)

One of the rewards of having climbed Ben More is the knowledge that in Britain south of this point there is no loftier perch. Unfortunately, a shameful band of litter-spreading hill-goers have paid homage to its status in blatant disregard for the mountain environment.

Leave the triangulation pillar by means of the unmistakable path that goes down steeply on the south side. In places, the erosion is severe but there is only one awkward outcrop, just below the summit, that requires a little extra care with the footwork. At the Bealach-eadar-dha Beinn begins the last of the climbing, not only of the day but, for those following the Round, of the fortnight. It will undoubtedly prove a quite gruelling final pull up to the top on the steep twisting path.

From a distance Stob Binnein exhibits a distinctive wedge-shaped top. When you are on the summit it is evident that it is a narrow crest, 70m (230ft) or so in length. A cairn

Ben More (right) and Stob Binnein from Leskine, Glen Dochart.

OVERLEAF

has evolved at its southern extremity from where the mountains lying further S, such as Ben Lomond and the Arrochar Alps, are clearly visible. You may be joined here by Munroists ascending the Stob's southern ridge.

STOB BINNEIN TO CRIANLARICH
(Allow 3 hours)

Return to the Bealach-eadar-dha Beinn, and take the path on the left. Head out WNW, veering NW, across the flank of the hillside above Benmore Glen, to a point where the path fades to non-existence. From here, strike off W down the steep slope of the open hill, aiming for the southern edge of the plantation on the opposite bank of the Benmore Burn. Lower down, large areas of the hillside are prone to becoming waterlogged.

Near the bottom, a scattering of large boulders litters drier, more level ground, before you reach the track adjacent to a footbridge over the Benmore Burn. Keep to the east bank and continue the speedy descent N to Glen Dochart, enjoying here the good, dry track and the respite it brings. A series of hairpin bends brings the track down to Benmore Farm. Just before the farm, a stile on the right crosses the fencing at the roadside.

Follow the A85 W for 3km (2 miles) to reach Crianlarich. It is worth succumbing to the distraction of lovely Loch Dochart, before a well-deserved dram in the village.

> And the end of all our exploring
>
> will be to arrive where we started
>
> And know the place for the first time.

From *Little Gidding* by T.S. Eliot

ALTERNATIVE ROUTES
LOW-LEVEL OPTION VIA THE ALLT ESSAN
(Allow 4¼ hours)

From Luib continue beyond the Allt Coire Chaorach, leaving the A85 after a further 1km (⅔ mile). Take the minor road off to the right, towards Auchessan. At the bridge over the River Dochart there is a sign for the Auchessan Estate with the usual PR blurb, welcoming walkers but warning of high-velocity rifles during stalking.

Bear right in front of the estate buildings and go through a gate on the left. Once behind the last house, walk up beside the Allt Essan, adjacent to the top of a plantation on the opposite bank. Follow the rough path up along the course of the lively stream. Dense summer bracken might dictate a less obstructed course on the south bank.

There are fine views to enjoy as you look back down Glen Dochart and also the possibility of seeing red deer. The gently rising traverse westwards, over heathery tussocks, is not entirely stumble-free, but such moments are few in this tranquil if bleak landscape.

The positioning of new deer fencing might cause problems, but such obstacles may be avoided by skirting the fence perimeter located further N and S of the stream. For an update on the best course of action, contact the estate managers on (01567) 820421.

Having reached the source of the Allt Essan, at the loch of the same name, walk around its north side and leave the west shore on a bearing WSW (245° in mist), making for a point on the skyline to the right of visible fence posts. For a view over Strath Fillan, continue W of Loch Maragan and climb the heathery promontory at 514m (1,686ft), GR 398279. There is a rough path on its north side.

Walk W from the summit, veering NW, to reach the corner of a plantation forest by the Inverhaggernie Burn. Keeping to the plantation side, head downstream to pick up a track at the bottom by the farm at Inverhaggernie. An access road bridges the River Fillan before joining the A82. Crianlarich is now just a 2km (1¼ mile) roadside stroll away.

ESCAPES

The obvious curtailment of the main route is simply to omit the outlying peak of Stob Binnein. Descending to the Benmore Burn from the Bealach-eadar-dha Beinn, after reaching the summit of Ben More, results in a saving of about 1 hour.

As already noted, the most direct route between Ben More and Benmore Farm is via the mountain's northwestern slope, and this option provides the fastest retreat from its summit. However, as a means of ascent, if you have set off from Luib or the east side of Glen Dochart, this route has neither time- nor energy-saving advantages.

EXTENSIONS

Walkers wishing to prolong their final day on the Round can follow the ridge of the southern arm that demarcates the Coire Chaorach. From the top of the plantation, cross the Allt Coire Chaorach and ascend the northeastern ridge of Stob Creagach, continuing westwards up to Stob Binnein. Ben More is thus last in line and can be climbed before a return to, and a descent from, the Bealach-eadar-dha Beinn. Allow an extra 1¼ hours.

Loch Dochart.

OVERLEAF

APPENDIX 1

ACCOMMODATION REGISTER

Overnight Location	Hotel/Guest House OR Youth Hostel	Number of Rooms Single Double Twin Family	Charges B&B DB&B	Packed Lunch	Open	Comments
CRIANLARICH	CRIANLARICH YOUTH H. Station Road Crianlarich, Perthshire FK20 8QN Tel. (01838) 300260	76 Bunks in 13 dorms	6.50 N/A junior 7.75 senior	N/A	1 Feb–4 Jan	Grade 1 (superior) hostel. Modern building, with full facilities. Conveniently located near station and village.
	Carole & Peter Flockhart CRAIGBANK GUEST HSE Crianlarich, Perthshire FK20 8QS Tel. (01838) 300279	– 1 3 2	15–17 N/A	Y	All year	Friendly, welcoming house at E end of village, providing adequate, no fuss B&B – empathy with walkers' needs.
	GLENARDRAN GUEST HSE Crianlarich, Perthshire FK20 8QS Tel. (01838) 300236	4 en suite rooms	22.50 Dinner available	Y	All year	STB Three Stars. Unknown to author. Non-smoking.
	Ian & Jean Walker EWICH HOUSE Strathfillan, Crianlarich Perthshire FK20 8RU Tel. (01838) 300300	1 2 2 –	27.50 44.50	Y	All year	STB Three Stars. Unknown to author. Located 3km (2 miles) NW of village.

Overnight Location	Hotel/Guest House OR Youth Hostel	Number of Rooms Single Double Twin Family				Charges B&B	DB&B	Packed Lunch	Open	Comments
TYNDRUM	John & Barbara Riley INVERVEY HOTEL Tyndrum, Perthshire FK20 8RY Tel. (01838) 400219	5	5	7	4	20–28	30–4	Y	All year	STB 'Approved' hotel including 18 en suite rooms. Located at N end of village. Unknown to author.
	GLENGARRY GUEST HSE Tyndrum, Perthshire FK20 8RY Tel. (01838) 400224	–	1	1	1	15–18	Dinner available (prior booking only); enquire for prices	Y	Jan–Dec	STB 'Approved'. Fresh food claimed to be 'a speciality'. Unknown to author.
	Mrs Rena Baillie AUCHTERTYRE FARM Tyndrum, Crianlarich, Perthshire FK20 8RU Tel. (01838) 400251	2 bedrooms available				15	N/A	N/A	All year	Quiet location, 3km (2 miles) ESE of village also has 4 fully equipped 'wigwams' (all with electric light and heating) that accommodate 5 persons each at £8 per night (not including breakfast). Camping is available at £3 per person per night.
DALMALLY	Mr Cressey CRAIG VILLA GUEST HSE Dalmally, Argyll PA33 1AX Tel. (01838) 200255	–	2	2	2	19–23	30–35	Y	Apr–Oct	STB 'Commended'. Converted farmhouse. All rooms have en suite/private bathrooms. Unknown to author.

Overnight Location	Hotel/Guest House OR Youth Hostel	Number of Rooms Single Double Twin Family				Charges B&B	DB&B	Packed Lunch	Open	Comments
	Mrs M. MacDougall STRATHORCHY, Dalmally, Argyll PA33 1AE Tel. (01838) 200373	–	2	2	–	15–18	N/A	Y	All year	STB 'Commended'. Located on W side of village, meals available locally. Unknown to author.
	ORCHY BANK GUEST HSE Dalmally, Argyll PA33 1AS Tel. (01838) 200370	2	2	2	2	16–18	26–28	Y	All year	STB 'Commended'. Unknown to author
GLENCOE	KING'S HOUSE HOTEL Kingshouse, Glencoe Argyll PA39 4HY Tel. 01855 851259	21 bedrooms available, 12 en suite				From 23.50*	Dinner available; bar & restaurant menu	Y	All year	Conveniently located at the top of Glen Coe and Glen Etive; popular with walkers and climbers.
						*(Breakfast extra. Cont. 4.00, full 7.50)				
	Eileen, Peter, Guy & Edward Daynes CLACHAIG INN Glencoe, Argyll PA39 4HX Tel. (01855) 811252	2	5	7	5	19.50–31	Dinner available; à la carte/ bar & restaurant menu	Y	All year	STB One Star Inn. 16 rooms en suite. Adjoined to 'Best pub in Scotland'– very popular with walkers and climbers.
	GLENCOE YOUTH H Glencoe, Ballachulish Argyll PA39 4HX Tel. (01855) 811219	62 beds (dorms only)				6.95 (Cont. breakfast for groups only)	N/A	N/A	All year	Grade 1 (standard) hostel with all mod cons. Alpine cabin-type, amid superb scenery – located 2.4km (1½ miles) from village.

Overnight Location	Hotel/Guest House OR Youth Hostel	Number of Rooms Single Double Twin Family	Charges B&B	DB&B	Packed Lunch	Open	Comments
KINLOCHLEVEN	Mrs Elsie Robertson EDENCOILLE Garbien Road Kinlochleven, Argyll PA40 4SE Tel. (01855) 831358	1 1 1 –	16–20	Dinner available (enquire for prices)	Y	All year	STB Three Stars. Unknown to author.
	Mac Innes TAILRACE INN Riverside Road, Kinlochleven, Argyll PA40 4QH Tel. (01855) 831777	– 2 3 1 all en suite and with TVs	16–19.50	Dinner available; bar meals all day	Y	All year	Welcoming to walkers, with drying room, etc. Unknown to author. Also self-catering flats.
	Martin & Margaret Reece MACDONALD HOTEL Fort William Road Kinlochleven, Argyll PA40 4QL Tel. (01855) 831539	10 bedrooms available including en suite rooms	20–30	38–48 also bar menu	Y	Mar–Dec	Les Routiers and Consort appointed. Unknown to author.
	MAMORE LODGE HOTEL Kinlochleven, Argyll PA40 4QN Tel. (01855) 831213	17 bedrooms available, and 1 bunkhouse	from 18	Dinner available; bar menu	Y	All year	B&B in hotel annexe as well as bunkhouse accommodation.
GLEN NEVIS	GLEN NEVIS YOUTH H. Glen Nevis Fort William Inverness-shire PH33 6ST Tel. (01397) 702336	123 beds (including 6 family rooms)	8.64 over 18s. (Cont. breakfast £2)	N/A	2.15	All year	Grade 1 (superior) hostel with all mod cons. Mountain cabin-type, next to beautiful River Nevis. Very convenient for the Ben.
	Maurice & Dianne Young ACHINTEE FARM GUEST H. Glen Nevis Fort William Inverness-shire PN33 6TE Tel. (01397) 702240	5 bedrooms available	18–22	N/A		All year	STB 'Commended'. Distinctive early 19th-century house. Ideally located for Ben Nevis.
	ACHINTEE BUNKHOUSE (as above)	20 bunk beds in 1 dorm (all curtained). Bedding supplied.	8 (no break-fast)	N/A		All year	Basic accommodation, full self-catering facilities.

OVERNIGHT Location	Hotel/Guest House OR Youth Hostel	Number of Rooms Single Double Twin Family	Charges B&B	DB&B	Packed Lunch	Open	Comments
LOCH OSSIAN	LOCH OSSIAN YOUTH H. Corrour (S.O.) by Fort William Inverness-shire PH30 4AA Tel. (01397) 732207	20 bunk beds in 2 dorms	4.65 (no break-fast)	N/A	N/A	End Mar–end Oct	Grade 3 (simple) hostel; A remote get-away-from-it-all hostel. Bring own food supplies. Home of 'run around the loch in under the hour club'.
	Angela Brown CORROUR STATION BUNKHOUSE Corrour Station, by Fort William Inverness-shire PH30 Tel. (01397) 732236	14 bunk beds in total. Bedding supplied.	5.50	N/A	N/A	All year	Quiet location by the platform of a remote station on the edge of Rannoch Moor. Sells food. Advance booking advisable.
BRIDGE OF GAUR	Mrs Robertson CAMUSERICHT FARM Bridge of Gaur Perthshire PH17 Tel. (01882) 633219	2/3 bedrooms sleeping up to 6 in total	15	21 (prior booking only)	Y	April–Oct	Working house in idyllic rural setting. No luxuries but hearty grub like grandma used to make! Located just N of Br. of Gaur.
RANNOCH	MOOR OF RANNOCH HOTEL Rannoch Station Perthshire PH17 2QA Tel. (01882) 633238	– 3 2 1	25	Dinner available; bar and restaurant menu	Y	All year	Located opposite Rannoch station; an alter-native when Camusericht Farm is full or between Oct & May. Unknown to author.
GLEN LYON	Mrs Hardy INVERVAR LODGE Glen Lyon, Aberfeldy Perthshire PH15 2PL Tel. (01887) 877206	– 1 1 1	24–30	39–45	Y	Jan–Dec	Typical Scottish estate lodge style, in beautiful setting. Comfortable rooms, good facilities and stacks of food!

Overnight Location	Hotel/Guest House OR Youth Hostel	Number of Rooms Single Double Twin Family				Charges B&B	DB&B	Packed Lunch	Open	Comments
GLEN LYON cont.	Mrs K.A. Conway GLEN LYON P.O. Bridge of Balgie Glen Lyon, Aberfeldy Perthshire PH15 2PP Tel. (01887) 866221	–	–	–	1	12–18	Dinner available only in winter (prior booking only); enquire for prices	Y	All year except Christmas and New Year	Room comes with sitting room. Unknown to author.
KILLIN	Killin Youth H. Killin Perthshire FK21 8TN Tel/Fax (01567) 820546	46 bunk beds in 5 dorms (includes one 4-bed and one 6-bed family room)				6.10	N/A	N/A	Feb–Nov	Grade 2 (limited access) hostel. Attractive stone building with good facilities including new toilet-shower block (with disabled toilet). Convenient for village services.
	Frank & Margaret Ogilvie BRIDGE OF LOCHAY HOTEL Killin Perthshire FK21 8TS Tel. (01567) 820272	All rooms en suite				23	33 also bar menu and à la carte menu	Y	All year	Attractive exterior in lovely spot at N end of village (near YH).
	CRAIGBUIE GUEST HSE Main Street, Killin Perthshire FK21 8UH Tel. (01567) 820439	–	2	2	3	16–20	No dinner available	Y	Jan–Nov	Good value for money B&B in a Victorian villa in the village centre.
GLEN DOCHART	Tam Bolton LUIB HOTEL Crianlarich Perthshire FK20 8QT Tel. (01567) 820664	–	2	1	2	17.50	Dinner available; bar and restaurant menu	Y	All year	Average hotel with friendly landlord and pleasantly located in rural Glen Dochart. Cosy atmosphere.
	SUIE LODGE HOTEL Glendochart, Crianlarich Perthshire FK20 8QT Tel. (01567) 820417	1	4	4	2	17–22	Dinner available; enquire for prices	Y	All year	STB 'Approved' hotel including en suite rooms.

Appendix 2

Useful Addresses

Argyll, the Isles, Loch Lomond, Stirling & Trossachs Tourist Board
Old Town Jail
St John Street
Stirling FK8 1EA
tel: 01786 470945

Association for the Protection of Rural Scotland
Gladstone's Land (3rd floor)
483 Lawnmarket
Edinburgh EH1 2NT
tel: 0131 225 7012/3

Forestry Commission
231 Corstorphine Road
Edinburgh EH12 7AT
tel: 0131 334 0303

Fort William and Lochaber Tourist Board
Cameron Square
Fort William PH33 6AJ
tel: 01397 703781

Highlands of Scotland Tourist Board
Peffery House
Strathpeffer
IV14 9HA
tel: 01997 421160

Historic Scotland
Longmore House
Salisbury Place
Edinburgh EH9 1SH
tel: 0131 668 8600

John Muir Trust
41 Commercial Street
Leith, Edinburgh EH6 6JD
tel: 0131 554 0114

The Mountaineering Council of Scotland
4a St Catherine's Road
Perth PH1 5SE
tel: 01738 638227

Midland Bluebird
(for bus service to Crianlarich)
Stirling
tel: 01324 623901

National Coach Services Enquiry Line
National Express
tel: 0990 808080

National Trust for Scotland
5 Charlotte Square
Edinburgh EH2 4DU
tel: 0131 226 5922

Ordnance Survey (OS)
Grayfield House
5 Bankhead Avenue
Edinburgh EH11 4AE
tel: 0131 442 3985

Post-bus
(for timetables)
Royal Mail Public Relations Office
Edinburgh
tel: 0131 228 7407

Ramblers' Association Scotland
Crusader House
Haig Business Park
Markinch, Fife KY7 6AQ
tel: 01592 611 177

Royal Society for the Protection of Birds (RSPB)
Scottish Headquarters
17 Regent Terrace
Edinburgh EH7 5BN
tel: 0131 557 3136

Scotrail Customer Services
(for Edinburgh, Glasgow, West Highland line services etc.)
tel: 0141 3354612

Train information
tel: 0345 484950

Scottish Avalanche Information Service (SAIS)
Police/SAIS Avalanche Information Line
tel: 01479 861264

Scottish Countryside Activities Council
23 Lochardil Place
Inverness IV2 4LN
tel: 01463 235720

Scottish Landowners Federation
25 Maritime Street
Leith
Edinburgh EH6 5PW
tel: 0131 555 1031

Scottish Natural Heritage (SNH)
12 Hope Terrace
Edinburgh EH9 2AS
tel: 0131 447 4784

Scottish Rights of Way Society
John Cotton Business Centre
10 Sunnyside
Edinburgh EH7 5RA
tel: 0131 652 2937

Scottish Sports Council
Caledonia House
South Gyle
Edinburgh EH12 9DQ
tel: 0131 317 7200

Scottish Tourist Board
23 Ravelston Terrace
Edinburgh EH4 3EU
tel: 0131 332 2433

Scottish Wildlife Trust (SWT)
Cramond House
Cramond Glebe Road
Edinburgh EH4 6NS
tel: 0131 312 7765

Scottish Youth Hostels Association (SYHA)
7 Glebe Crescent
Stirling FK8 2JA
tel: 01786 451181

INDEX